Dynamics of Personal Growth

Dynamics of Personal Growth

Fakir M. Sahoo

Formerly Professor & Head
Centre of Advanced Study in Psychology
Utkal University, Bhubaneswar, India
(Now at, XIM University, Bhubaneswar)

Black Eagle Books
2022

Black Eagle Books
USA address:
7464 Wisdom Lane
Dublin, OH 43016

India address:
E/312, Trident Galaxy, Kalinga Nagar,
Bhubaneswar-751003, Odisha, India

E-mail: info@blackeaglebooks.org
Website: www.blackeaglebooks.org

First International Edition Published by
Black Eagle Books, 2022

DYNAMICS OF PERSONAL GROWTH
by **Fakir Mohan Sahoo**

Copyright © **Fakir Mohan Sahoo**

All rights reserved. No part of this publication may be reproduced, stored in a retrieval system, or transmitted, in any form or by any means, electronic, mechanical, photocopying, recording or otherwise without the prior permission of the publisher.

Cover & Interior Design: Ezy's Publication

ISBN- 978-1-64560-302-3 (Paperback)
Library of Congress Control Number: 2022944719

Printed in the United States of America

To management students at XIMB/XIM whose questions / queries and interactions have broadened the contours of my exploration and exposition.

FMS

CONTENTS

PART-1: CORE CONCERNS

Chapter 1: Combating Helplessness — 15
 Helplessness Syndrome
 Explanatory Styles
 Combating Skills

Chapter 2: Building Self-Efficacy — 21
 Sources of Self-Efficacy
 Mediating Mechanisms
 Psychological Well-Being
 Career Choice and Development
 Self-Efficacy and Leadership
 Tips for Training

Chapter 3: Promoting Optimism — 41
 Nature of Optimism
 Optimism in Workplace
 Training for Optimism

Chapter 4: Fostering Resilience — 45
 Features of Resilience
 Training of Resilience

Chapter 5: Emotional Intelligence — 50
 Evolution of the Construct
 IQ and EQ
 Significance of EI

Chapter 6: Stimulating Hope — 59
 Parameters of Hope
 Antecedents of Hope

Chapter 7: Flow — 62
 Flow Experience
 Contours of Flow
 Support System

Chapter 8:	Work Life Integration	71
	Conceptual Framework	
	Measurement Issues	
	Antecedents of Conflict	
	Consequences of Conflict	
	Work-Family Facilitation	
Chapter 9:	Workplace Spirituality	89
	Defining Spirituality	
	Spiritual Intelligence	
	Scientific Evidence	
	Operational Parameters	
	Pragmatic Strategies	
	Spiritual Leader	
Chapter 10:	Androgyny and Work Behaviour	105
	Traditional View of Gender Stereotypes	
	Measurement	
	Androgyny and Behavioural Flexibility	
	Androgyny and Work Involvement	
	Appendix (SSRI)	
Chapter 11:	Workplace Well-Being	117
	Predictors of Well-Being	
	Process Nature of Well-Being	
	Workplace Well-Being	

PART 2: SUPPLEMENTARY READINGS

Chapter 12:	Creativity	137
	Training for Creativity	
	The Creative Process	
	Phases of Creative Process	
	Relevant Factors	
Chapter 13:	Harnessing the Science of Emotion	158
	Landmarks in Emotion Research	
	Major Principles	
Chapter 14:	Savouring	177

Chapter 15:	Empathy Dynamics of Empathy Contributors to Empathy Development	180
Chapter 16:	Attitude of Gratitude Practice of Gratitude	190
Chapter 17:	Building Flourishing Relationship Passionate and Compassionate Aspect The Triangular Component The Self-Expansion of Romantic Love	195
Chapter 18:	Spirituality Defining Spirituality The Discovery of the Sacred	202
Chapter 19:	Meditation The Process The Techniques	205
Chapter 20:	On Inspiration Characteristics of Inspired People Inspiration and Creativity Increasing Wellness	208
Chapter 21:	Performance Excellence	212
Chapter 22:	Seeking Uniqueness	215
Chapter 23:	Cultural Intelligence	218
Chapter 24:	Forgiveness	221
Chapter 25:	Humility	226
Chapter 26:	Rewire Your Brain The Cortical Representation Towards Plasticity Notion Therapeutic Application	230
Recommended Readings		239

Books Authored by F.M. Sahoo

- Cognitive styles & amp; interpersonal behaviour
- Affective sensitivity & amp; cognitive styles
- Psychology in Indian context (Edited)
- Environment & amp; behaviour
- Child rearing & amp; educating assistance manual
- Dynamics of human helplessness
- Sex roles in transition
- Behavioural issues in ageing (Edited)
- Atlas of mind
- Mysteries of mind
- Wonders of mind
- Splendours of mind
- Mind management
- Tools of mind
- Landscape of mind
- Plasticity of mind
- Melody of Minds
- Happiness flows
- Dynamics of Personal Growth
- Essentials of Employee Counselling

Books in Odia

- Bichitra mana
- Manasika bikruti
- Jiban prabahare manasika bikruti
- Adhuni ka jibanare manasika chapa
- Manara manachitra
- Manastatvika bikasare saisaba parba
- Byaktitva & amp; netrutva
- Nari manastatva
- Manastatvika bikasara godhuli parba
- Sisu manara bigyan
- Sachitra mana
- Sabala mana, saphala jibana
- Manastatvika bikasara balya parba
- Manastatvika bikasara kaishore parba
- Manasika samasya O samadhan
- Manara rahasya
- Jibana O' manastatwa
- Tallinata
- Sahitya O' manastatwa
- Chapamukta jeeban
- Sakshyatakara
- Manastatwika bikashar jouban parba
- Sukhanubhutira marmakatha
- Mana Prikrama
- Manara Bhugola

Translation

- Divya Sambasana (Part-v)
- Divya Sambasana (Part-xv)
- Shiridi ru Puttaparti
- Siksha Samparkare
- Bibeka Sampritee
- Chetanadipta Jiban
- Dhyanadipta Jiban

Preface

The growth and development in any sector requires a multi–strategy approach. Irrespective of the levels of strategy operation, the person constitutes the core concern. Although it is relatively easy to change material environment with application of science and technology, the process of altering human element poses a formidable challenge.

Fortunately, psychological science aided by recent discoveries in neuroscience has provided immense help for harnessing human potential. More specifically the recent developments in positive psychology with its emphasis on the slogan "build health" (instead of 'fight disease') have reoriented our efforts to make the best possible use of psychological capital.

The book "Dynamics of Human Growth" presents an essential introduction to the area of positive behaviour. While it meets academic requirements of management students and scholars, it offers enriching and elevating materials for students and scholars in allied disciplines as well as general readers. I thank Black Eagle Publication for their helpful considerations.

13 July 2022   **F. M. Sahoo**
Guru Poornima

PART-1
CORE CONCERNS

Chapter 1

Combating Helplessness

Every one desire success but a few individuals persist in their attempt to bring success. There is a wide variation in the individual difference in persistence. While failures discourage many people, failures may also help other people to intensify their efforts and accomplish success in the long run. The adverse effect of helplessness has prompted us to ponder over its dynamics and the remediation.

Helplessness Syndrome

The initial clues regarding its dynamics came from experimental psychologists. A renowned psychologist Martin Seligman was conducting learning experiments on rats in the University of Pennsylvania. He came across an interesting observation. He observed behaviour of rats on a platform. The platform has two compartments; one was safe and the other was unsafe. The arrangement was such that the rat would experience mild electric shock while on the unsafe compartment. An one would easily figure out the rat would move to the safe one following the experience of shock. The rat developed the skill of avoiding the shock by moving to the safe compartment.

The experimenter was curious to know the consequences of making both platforms unsafe. When both sides were electrically charged, the rat made initial attempts to avoid the shock by moving back and forth. Soon it found that there was no escape. Subsequently, it reduced its random activity, it stayed in a particular place. Surprisingly enough it did not make any attempt to escape the shock even it the other compartment was made safe. The animal showed all forms of passivity.

Similar experiments were conducted on other animals as well. Findings were supportive. Experiments on humans demonstrated similar consequences. Humans were given unsolvable puzzles to work with. Subsequently they were given solvable puzzle without being informed that a change was introduced. It was found that people experiencing initial helplessness showed "give-up" responses. Some of studies led to the conclusion that helplessness develops when people perceive the response outcome independence. In other words, the perception of uncontrollability is at the root of helplessness.

Once developed, helplessness generates four consequences. Deficits are noticed in four areas: learning, motivation, feeling, and self-confidence. First, helplessness adversely affects acquisition of new skills. When individuals perceive that there is no connection between response and outcomes, they stop forming new associations. For example, a worker may experience the lack of connection between his/her efforts and positive outcome (promotion). The repetition of such experience would induce him/her not to acquire the skill of hard work (effort). Similarly, a student's observation that his/her behaviour is unrelated to teacher's satisfaction would prevent him/her from new behaviours.

The second difficulty is manifest in motivational domain. Since past exercise has proved futile, individuals do not show initiation of responses. There would not be further initiatives. Physical activity, mental exploration and efforts would be reduced to the minimum. Third, there would be a feeling deficit. The helpless individuals show depressive postures. Their sad mood is reflected in physical withdrawal, reduced conversation, limited social interaction and loneliness.

Fourth deficit is manifest in case of humans only. The failure to solve the problem induces a sense of loss of worth. The individual loses self-esteem. The perception that there is no ability to control the environment leads to the loss of esteem.

Thus, helplessness manifests itself in the form of deficits in the areas of learning motivation, feeling, and self-esteem.

Explanatory Styles
It has been posited that a prolonged exposure to uncontrollable (bad) events generates helplessness deficits. Yet, a fundamental question is not resolved. All people exposed to similar amounts of uncontrollability (bad events) do not show equal amount of helplessness. What is the cause of this individual difference?

In recent years psychologists have provided some convincing answers. According to them, people ask *three* important questions to themselves when they encounter had events. The way they answer these questions determine their passivity.

The first question pertains to the cause of the bad event. Who is responsible for the negative events? Although all people ask themselves this question, they answer it differently. Some people use internal explanations, they think themselves to be the cause of the bad events. On the contrary, other people use external explanations, they consider others and outside circumstances to be the cause of the bad events. Needless to say, internality-externality is a continuum; individuals place themselves on specific points of this continuum. It can be easily shown that persons employing extreme internal explanation have intense guilt and self-blame. Consequently, their helplessness is intense, since they view failure as a resultant of their inability. They also experience intense self-esteem loss. Thus, internality is strongly associated with intense helplessness and a great deal of loss of self-esteem. On the contrary, the tendency to explain bad events in external terms protects the individual from experiencing heightened helplessness and intense self-esteem loss.

The second question people raise is related to the duration of bad events. How long would the events stay? People may use stable attribution; they may consider the event to be permanent. In this case, their helplessness would be long-lasting. On the contrary, other people may view the bad event is unstable. This would make helplessness short lived. Thus, the chronicity of helplessness syndrome depends in the stability explanation. If bad events are considered long lasting, helplessness tends to be chronic. If bad events are viewed temporary phenomena, helplessness is fragile.

Finally, people facing helplessness tend to ask another fundamental question: How pervasive is the effect of the event? For instance, a person sustains a hand injury. In the midst of such a bad event, the person may think that his or her life is doomed. This is a global explanation. The event has adversely affected his or her hand, but it is generalized to other areas of life. Another person in similar situation may think differently. He or she may think that his or her hand is injured, but many works can still be done. Other possibilities are open. This is a specific explanation. The individual is limiting the effect to the case of injured hand only. As one can surmize, globality of explanation leads to pervasiveness of negative effect. When global explanations are employed, negative effects appear in other domains of life. For instance, a person may experience a jolt in his or her interpersonal life. He or she may feel betrayed by a friend. With global explanation, the person would perculate it to work life. He or she would not trust his or her boss (in work setting) because of the generalization of effect from interpersonal domain to work domain.In contrast, an individual using specific attribution would limit to interpersonal domain only. The use of specific explanation would limit the effect to that specific domain where it originates. This would circumscribe the negative effect.

In sum, internality, stability and globality of explaining bad events increases intensity, chronicity and generality of helplessness. On the contrary externality, instability and specificity reduce the negative consequences.

Combating Skills

The foregoing discussion amply illustrates the significance of explanatory styles. Yet, nothing is said with respect to explaining good (positive) events.

Studies have shown that people could also adopt optimistic explanatory styles while explaining good events. An optimistic approach involves explaining good (positive) events in internal, stable, and global terms.

Internal explanation implies that the individual emphasizes his or her own role in the causation of positive event. The more individuals think of their roles and participation in the context of good events, their well-being is likely to be enhanced, it boosts self-confidence. On the contrary, the thought that a positive event has been caused by external circumstances would not contribute towards individual's wellness.

Similarly, individuals ought to use stable explanations for good events. Instead of considering the event to be temporary they should view it as a long-lasting phenomenon. When they stretch it over time, their pleasure also becomes long-lasting. If a good event has happened today, it is better to think of it tomorrow, day after tomorrow, and many days, weeks and months following the event.

Finally, an individual needs to generalize the effects of positive events to other areas of life. If a good thing happens in interpersonal domain (such as deep appreciation by a friend), the individual will feel better when it is spilled into work life. Similarly, the effects of good happenings in the work setting may be spread to interpersonal life. The globality as opposed to specificity is useful in spreading good consequences.

In sum, we would be better-off if we explain good events using internal stable and global factors. Thus, optimistic explanatory styles are needed both at the time of explaining bad events as well as good events.

As aspect of helplessness is the cognitive expectancy. It is the expectation of no control that initially plants the seed of helplessness. Consequently, the individual must overcome a sense of uncontrollability. A sense of controllability accompanied with optimistic explanatory styles as outlined is a surer protection against helplessness.

Chapter 2

Building Self–Efficacy

People's beliefs about their capabilities to produce outcomes define perceived self- efficacy. Self–efficacy beliefs determines how people feel, think, motivate themselves and behave.

A strong sense of efficacy enhances human achievement and personal well–being in many ways. People with high efficacy approach difficult tasks as challenges to be mastered rather than as threats to be avoided. Such an efficacious approach fosters intrinsic interest and deep involvement in activities. They set challenging goals and develop commitment to goals. They heighten and sustain their efforts in the face of failure. They attribute failure to insufficient efforts or flawed strategy. On the other hand, people with doubts about their capabilities avoid difficult tasks. They display low aspiration and weak commitment. They fall easy victims to stress and depression.

Albert Bandura (1997) has developed a robust theoretical framework of self- efficacy. In the recent years, measurement techniques have been developed, its sources have been identified, mediating mechanisms have been delineated, and their applications to various domains have been explicated.

Forms and Measurements

The concept of self–efficacy has been assessed in four different ways. First, it is expressed as a global personal construct, generalized over several domains. This personal *generalized self-efficacy* represents the extent of belief or capabilities in general. The second one is a *domain – specific* measurement. For instance, it is possible to measure teaching efficacy or swimming efficacy or child management efficacy or driving efficacy. Third, it is also possible to operationalize self-efficacy in a very specific task context such as self–efficacy to solve algebra problems. This is task specific efficacy. It is obvious that behavioural prediction would become more and more accurate as we move from generalized to *task–specific self-efficacy*.

Self–efficacy could be set up for each of the major tasks. This scale would include, in ascending order, items that represent the increasing level of difficulty. The respondent would check for each item yes or no (magnitude) and then next to 0 – 100% probability or attainment (i.e. strength). *Figure 1 shows such a scale.* The efficacy scores are derived be getting a total of probability strengths for each item with yes. This composite method is shown to be valid as a reliable measure.

Figure 1: An Illustration of Measurement

Number of Car Sells per month	Yes or No	Certainty (0 – 100%)
I believe I can sell 2		
I believe I can sell 4		
I believe I can sell 6		
I believe I can sell 8		
I believe I can sell 10		
I believe I can sell 12		
I believe I can sell 14		
I believe I can sell 16		

In addition to three forms of self–efficacy, Bandura also stresses the significance of *collective efficacy*. For example, teachers' belief in their personal efficacy affects their general orientation towards the educational process as well as their instructional activity. At the same time, teachers operate collectively within an interactive social system rather than as isolates. Schools in which the staffs collectively judge themselves as capable of getting difficult students achieve academic success convey a group sense of accomplishment. Teachers with collective efficacy are likely to succeed in floating a new course of study and bringing need reformation. However, a robust method of measuring collective efficacy does not exist. Yet, it is asserted that collective efficacy is a stable predictor of social and organizational change.

In recent years, researchers have moved away from larger social aggregates to focus instead more narrowly on task–specific performance beliefs held by small groups. They have group efficacy. For example, Parker (1994) found that an aggregated individual's beliefs that group could achieve multiple levels of performance on a particular test were strong predictor of test performance.

However, the term group efficacy denotes emphasis on workgroups – a small number of interdependent members having a sense of themselves as a social unit with ongoing interaction.

Group efficacy contributes to successfully outcome through casual routes. First goal clarity is related to group efficacy. When a belief is well calibrated, a group with high group efficacy is able to mobilize the motivation, cognitive resources and courses of action needed to exercise control over critical strategic events in the environment. Briefly stated, it is suggested that members' efficacy, cohesiveness of the group and belief salience (belief in the importance of group goal) lead to group efficacy. Group efficacy facilitated by goal clarity, belief sharedness and environmental stability generate high level of performance (Gibson & Early 2002)

Sources of Self–efficacy

Peoples' belief about their efficacy can be developed by five main sources of influence. The most effective way of creating a strong sense of efficacy is through mastery experiences. Individuals need to broaden the range of their experiences. Students who expose themselves to new kinds of experimental exercise expand their self–efficacy. Teachers who enthusiastically participate in extra–institutional seminars, workshops, conferences and orientation progarmmes build stronger self-efficacy. Persons who eagerly venture out novel avenues of work experience acquire an enhanced self-efficacy. Developing a sense of efficacy through mastery experiences is not a matter of adopting ready made habits. It involves acquiring the cognitive, behavioural and self- regulatory tools creating and executing appropriate courses of action to manage ever–changing life circumstances.

The second effective way of creating and strengthening efficacy belief is *through intelligent structuring of initial experiences*. If people experience only easy success they come to expect quick results and are discouraged by failures. If people undertake very difficult tasks in the beginning, repeated failures may induce a sense of helplessness. In such circumstances, they become frustrated and dejected. Hence an intelligent strategy is to structure *initial experiences with task of moderate difficulty level*. Such an attempt is likely to bring about many successes, not all success, and a few failures. Attempts to overcome obstacles through perseverant effort would be helpful in building self-efficacy. Once strengthened, subsequent encounters with very difficult tasks would not pose problem from the viewpoint of enhancing self-efficacy. For building efficacy, positive experience with mastering task of moderate difficulty is valuable.

The third source of influence involves the vicarious experiences provided by role models. The impact of modeling on personal self efficacy is well documented. However, a subtle element seems to operate in this context. Individuals may identify appropriate role model. Yet they may not feel like imitating them. They may adore them. But they may not modify their own behaviours. Individuals basically perceive the distance between their role model and themselves. They may argue within themselves that their role model has been successful because of certain unique advantages. They, on the contrary, are in the midst of great difficulty. Such a perception creates a gap. Although they admire the role model, they are not strongly motivated to imitate them.

The impact of modeling on perceived self-efficacy is strongly influenced by perceived similarity to model. The greater the assumed similarity the more persuasive the models' success. Individuals develop self-persuasion on the basis of consideration that if they have difficulties, the models must be having some difficulties. If the models have some advantages they also have some advantages. This kind of perception reduces the gap between themselves and the models, it enhances similarity. If people see the models as similar to themselves, they are strongly motivated to imitate. The more similar the model (e.g. demographic such as age, physical characteristics, and education as well as status and education) and the more relevant the task being performed), more effect there will be on the observers' efficacy processing. They accept the role model as source of information as well as source of inspiration.

As a source of information models emit cues of capabilities. People observe competent models and gain knowledge regarding skillful behaviour. They observe models' behaviour pattern with respect to communication, skill execution, problem–solving and coping mechanisms. Undaunted attitudes exhibited by perseverant models in situations of obstructions transmit enabling cues. Apart from being a source of information, role models transmit inspiration to individuals. This enhances the arousal level of people in the directions of goal setting and accomplishment.

Social persuasion is a fourth way of strengthening people's self–efficacy beliefs. People who are persuaded verbally that they possess the capability to master given activities are likely to mobilize greater effort and sustain it. In contrast, they encounter problems if they harbor self – doubts and dwell on personal deficits. Social persuasion produces positive results when people use it extensively as efficacy–builders for a group of followers. For example, teachers can make use of social persuasion for themselves as well as for their students. Parents can use it for themselves and for their children. Managers and leaders can also use persuasive boosts for themselves and for their subordinates. "You can do it" - the repetition of this persuasive message with a strong force of conviction seems to promote development of skills in a desired direction.

Figure 2: Sources of Self–efficacy

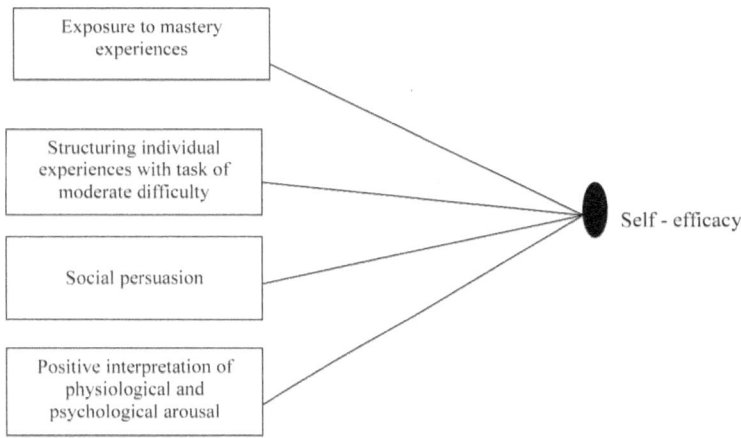

On the other hand, there is powerful effect of unkind words and negative feedback (e.g., "you can't do that"). However, it is not suggested that efficacy builders need to convey unrealistic praises. In addition to raising people's belief in their capabilities, they need to structure situations for them in ways that bring success and avoid placing people in situations where they are likely to fail often.

The fifth source of influence involves physiological and psychological arousal. People often rely on how they feel physiologically and emotionally, in order to assess their capability. If these sources of information give out negative signals the negative interpretation greatly distract from efficacy. When people feel they are tired or depressed or they are unwell, they do not feel themselves efficacious. The external conditions remaining constant, the interpretation may vary across persons. For instance, a day long hard work may prompt two different persons in two different ways. One may say that he or she is very tired. The other may verbalize that the day has been fully utilized.

Thus the way people look at and interpret physiological arousal is important. People with high efficacy beliefs attach positive interpretation to their arousal even though normal physiological responses are naturally indicative of fatigue. In other words, people who have a high sense of efficacy are likely to view their state of arousal as an energizing facilitation of performance whereas those who beset by self–doubts regard their arousal as a debilitator.

Although these sources of influence provide inputs for building efficacy, how these effects are mediated to produce desired behaviour outcomes improves scientific understanding of the phenomenon.

Mediating Mechanisms

Efficacy beliefs regulate human performance through four major processes. They include cognitive, motivational, affective and selection processes. These processes do not operate in isolation; rather they operate in combination with other processes.

Cognitive Process. Human behaviour is purposive; it is goal–oriented. All activities are preceded by forethoughts. In case of self-efficacious individuals, purposive behaviour is regulated by effective preplanning and forethought. Efficacious individuals make extended self–appraisal of their capabilities and set valued goals. The higher the goal challenges people set for themselves, firmer is their commitment to the goal.

A major function of forethought is to predict events and to develop ways to control those outcomes. Efficacious persons visualize success scenarios that provide positive guides and supports for performance. For example, an executive working on a future project presentation may visualize the physical setting of he room where the presentation is to be made, the sitting arrangement of the audience, his or her position as a presenter, eye glances of the audience and his or her reciprocation in such setting.

The preplanning is done with respect to answering the questions and dealing with negative comments from the audience. Those who doubt their efficiency visualize their failure scenarios and dwell on many things that can go wrong. It is difficult to achieve much while fighting self – doubt.

Cognitive processing also requires that the person remains focused on task. When people deal with complex environmental demands, there are many distractions. A strong sense of self – efficacy is helpful for remaining task oriented in face of distractions. Failures and setbacks, (the lack of efficiency beliefs) bring errors in analytic thinking. Such inefficacious individuals become erratic in their thought process and lower their aspiration.

Motivational Process. Efficiency beliefs play a key role in the management of motivation. Most human motivation is cognitively generated. People motivate themselves and guide their behaviours appropriately by the exercise of forethoughts. They set goals, plan a course of action, mobilize resources and develop commitment to goal attainment.

Psychologists have identified some key elements in human motivation. It is observed that people with self–efficacy make use of these key elements in their self–regulation of motivation.

First, adaptive motivation has a distinctive style of casual attribution. People who regard themselves as highly efficacious attribute their failures to insufficient effort or adverse situational conditions. In contrast, those who regard themselves as inefficacious tend to attribute their failure to ability. It is important to note that insufficient effort is controllable factor. If a person has not extended sufficient effort this time, he/she can do it next time. On the other hand, ability is very difficult to change. Casual attribution in terms of controllable factors facilitates accomplishment.

Second outcome–expectancy linkage is a seminal concept. In expectancy–value theory, motivation is determined by the expectation that a given course of behaviour will produce certain outcomes and the value placed on those outcomes. An efficacious student values the academic success and believes that there is a strong positive association between his/her learning and academic success. Similarly, an efficacious teacher attaches importance to students' acquisition of skills and believes that his or her teaching will certainly result in students' acquisition of skill. The motivating influence of outcome expectancies is well–documented. There are a large number of behavioural options which people do not undertake primarily because they do not consider the consequences of such behaviour as important and they are not very sure that behaviour would lead to expected outcomes.

The third element in the management of motivation concerns *goal setting*. A large body of evidence shows that explicit, challenging goals enhance and sustain motivation. Motivation-based goal setting involves a process of cognitive comparison of perceived performance to an adopted personal standard. By making self-satisfaction conditional or matching the standard, people give direction to their behaviour and create incentives to persist in their efforts until they fulfill their goals. They seek self–satisfaction from fulfilling valid goals. They are prompted to intensify their efforts by discontent with substandard performance.

According to Bandura, self–efficacious people

exercise three types of self-influences to manage their motivation in the context of goal attainment. First, they exercise self–satisfying and self–dissatisfying reactions to one's performance. When they meet high standards of performance, they feel happy. When their performance results in a substandard product, they are discontented. Second, they make use of self- monitoring. They make periodic assessment of their progress toward the goal. What is the nature of the goals? How much progress has been registered? What are the obstacles encountered? Similar evaluations are attempted. Third, they make readjustments of their personal goals based on one's progress.

When faced with obstacles and failure people who distrust their capabilities slacken their efforts and give up quickly. Those who have strong belief in their capabilities exert greater efforts. When they fail to master their challenge, strong perseverance contributes to performance accomplishment.

Affective Process. People's belief in their coping capabilities helps in the management of their negative emotion. Pervaded self–efficacy to exercise *control over stressor* plays a central role. People who believe that potential threats are unmanageable view many aspects of their environment as fraught with danger. They dwell on their coping deficiencies. They magnify the severity of their possible threats and worry about things that rarely happen. In contrast, people with efficacy belief construe their environment in an adaptive way.

The exercise of control over ruminative, disturbing thoughts is a second way in which efficacy beliefs regulate anxiety arousal and depression. It has been aptly said "you cannot prevent the birds of worry and care from flying over your head. But you can stop them from building a nest in your hair". It is not sheer frequency of disturbing thoughts but the perceived inability to turn them off that is the major source of distress. Hence both perceived self–efficacy and thought control efficacy operate jointly to reduce stress.

Third, social support reduces vulnerability to stress, depression and physical illness. Social support is not a self–forming entity. People have to go out and find or create supportive social relationships. This requires a strong sense of social efficacy. Supportive social support systems function very well in reducing vulnerability to depression. People with high social efficacy are insulated from vulnerabilities.

Adaptive Benefits of Efficacy Beliefs

There is a growing body of evidence that human accomplishment and personal well–being require an optimistic sense of personal efficacy. This is because ordinary social realities present difficulties and obstacles. In the midst of difficulties, realists forsake them, abandon their efforts prematurely or become cynical about the prospect of success. In contrast, people with a robust sense of personal efficacy continue with preserverant effort needed to succeed.

The adaptive benefits are pronounced in two major domains of human functioning: psychological well–being and performance accomplishment.

Psychological Well- Being

It is generally believed that misjudgment bring personal problem. However, the functional value of accurate self–appraisal depends on the nature of activity. Activities in which mistakes can produce costly consequences call for accurate judgment. It is a different matter elsewhere when people overestimate their capability, this functions as a creative illusion ever if this is an illusion. If efficacy beliefs reflect only what people can do routinely, they would rarely fail but they would not set aspirations beyond their immediate reach. They would not undertake extra effort needed to surpass, their ordinary performance.

The finding often shows that normal people are distorters of reality. They display self – enhancing biases and distort in the positive direction. People who are socially anxious or susceptible to depression are as socially skilled as those who do not suffer. But the normal ones believe that they are much more adept than they really are.

People with personal efficacy are also adept in changing their health practices. If doctor suggests them something and they decide to carry out. In contrast inefficacious individuals find it difficult to carry out unpleasant health programs. Thus, self-efficacy has a significant health – promotive role.

Human Accomplishment

Innovative achievements require resilient sense of efficacy. Social reformers strongly believe that they can mobilize the collective effort needed to bring social change. Although their beliefs are seldom fully realized, they sustain efforts. They adapt to existing realities. But those with a tenacious self-efficacy are likely to change those realities.

Similarity innovations require heavy investment of efforts over a long period with uncertain results. Moreover, innovations may clash with existing practices and preferences. This generates negative social reaction. Accordingly, one rarely finds realists in he ranks of innovators and great achievers.

In a delightful book titled *Rejection,* John White provides a convincing documentation of characteristics of people who have achieved eminence. They display a very high level of personal efficacy. They strongly believe in what they are doing. However, their resilient belief system enabled them to overcome repeated early rejection of their work. White cites the case of famous poet, James Joyce, whose book *Dubliners* was rejected by 22 publishers. The rejections of poems, musical compositions, scientific inventions and other products during he early phase of a celebrity is a normal phenomenon.

In essence, efficacious individuals harbor illusion about their capabilities and this helps them to go beyond the realistic bounds of achievement.

Implications for the Workplace

The scope of self-efficacy is no longer limited to changing behaviours in clinical setting. The concepts is applied to a wide variety of areas including the promotion of health and recovery from physical setbacks, the control of eating, resistance to addictive substances, educational achievement, athletic performance and importantly performance work settings.

Stajkovic and Luthans (2003) report the results of 114 studies and 21,616 participants. The results indicated a highly significant association between self-efficacy and job performance. Self–efficacy accounted for 28 percent increase in performance. In contrast, goal setting explained 10.39%, feedback explained 13.6% and organizational behaviour modification explained 17% of performance increments. Self-efficacy was also a better predictor compared with personality traits (e.g. the Big Five) and attitudes (e.g. job satisfaction or organizational commitment).

The considerable body of theory and research on self- efficacy has identified some specific domains of applications.

Career Choice and Development

Research findings strongly suggest that efficacy beliefs not only exert a strong direct influence on career decision making and career choice but self-efficacy also significantly influences the development of core vocational choice predictors such as interest, values and goals. The problem of underutilization of women's talents and abilities in career pursuits and the underrepresentation of women in higher status positions and occupations has long been a concern of vocational theorists. Hackett (1981) found that career efficiency beliefs play amore powerful role than interest, values and abilities in the restriction of women's career choices. Traditionally feminine sex-typed experiences in childhood often limit women's exposure to the sources of information necessary for the development of strong beliefs of efficacy. Lowered perceived efficacy along important career related dimensions could unduly restrict the types of occupations considered, Hackett also found no significant gender differences emerged when nontraditional and traditional occupations were examined separately. College-men's occupational self-efficacy was equivalent across occupations but women's occupational self-efficacy was significantly lower that men's for traditionally male-dominated occupations and significantly higher for traditionally female-dominated occupations.

Several elements of effective career decision making have been identified. These include goal selection, career exploration, problem solving capabilities, planning skills and realistic self- appraisal skills. Taylor and Betz (1983) developed the Career Decision Making Self–efficacy (CDMSE) scale to assess perception of efficacy with regard to these five dimensions. Research finding largely supported the usefulness of CDMSE scale in predicting career decision.

One of the benefits to counselors of career self-efficacy is that it provides guidelines for intervening to correct detrimental self beliefs. The four major sources of efficacy building performance accomplishment, vicarious learning, physiological arousal and affective states, and verbal persuasion, all provide means whereby unrealistic efficacy beliefs can be modified.

Self- Efficacy and Performance

Self-efficacy has a very well-established body of knowledge as to its applicability and positive impact on work- related performance. Luthans reported meta–analysis that included 114 studies and 21,616 subjects. The results indicated a highly significant correlation between self-efficacy and work-related performance. There was a 28 percent increase in performance due to self- efficacy. In contrast, other variables such as goal setting (10.39%), feedback (13.6%) and behaviour modification (17%) revealed less increment.

However, a number of studies show that self-efficacy is a stronger predictor for simple task. Its relationship with complex task performance is modified by a few other factors. For example, Shea and Howell (2000) found efficacy–performance spirals. While studying the relationship between self-efficacy and performances, they found that the pattern of relationship does not proceed in a monotonic fashion. Task-feedback and task experience affected the occurrence of self corrections in the pattern of changes in self-efficacy and performance over time.

Creative Performance

The concept of self-efficacy holds much promise for understanding creative action in organization setting. In fact, Ford (1996) placed self-efficacy belief as a key motivational component in his model of individual creative actions. Tierney and Farmer (2002) tested a new construct "creative self-efficacy". It measures employees' belief that they can be creative in their work roles. Creative self-efficacy was defined as the belief that one has ability to produce creative outcomes. With the use of this new tool, the researchers examined several hypotheses.

Overall, their findings supported that a both personal and contextual factors come into play when employees formulate work related self-efficacy judgments. A core sense of job capability is important for creative efficaciousness in one's work. Job efficacy was the strongest predictor of creative efficacy. The findings also highlighted the importance of managers providing training and experience opportunities necessary for employees to develop the sense of general job mastery.

The job complexity creativity link is also supported. The message for managers is that designing jobs to be multi-faceted and to require flexibility and experimentation is a first step toward promoting stronger creative self-efficacy among employees. It appears that employees believe they have creative capability when they work with supervisors who build their confidence through verbal persuasion and serve as models for activities core to creative performance.

Self- efficacy and Leadership

As environments rapidly change, managers are being asked to respond by actively seeking out new opportunities and leading their followers to exploit them to full advantage. Puglis and Green (2002) developed a three dimensional constrict *Leadership Self efficacy* (LSE) to reflect managers' self perceived capability for successfully executing the behaviours required to effect change in workplace. The three dimensions included direction setting, gaining followers commitment, and overcoming obstacles to change.

Consistent with self-efficacy theory, the central hypothesis that high LSE manager would engage in more leadership attempts compared to self- doubters. Supportive findings were obtained. Direction setting and gaining commitment components of LSE were positively correlated with subordinate ratings of manager, leadership attempts. As for the third LSE dimension, overcoming obstacle, an interaction effect was found. This suggests that a high level of organizational commitment is necessary for manager's efficacy for overcoming obstacles to be translated into leadership action.

Several factors, both characteristics of the individual as well as features of the work context, were proposed as influences on managers LSE. Across several analyses, some of the most consistently significant result were obtained for self esteem, performance ability and job autonomy.

However, the significance of LSE must not be overstated. There is an acceptance that leadership effectiveness is contingent on a host of variables. Since leadership fundamentally refers to relationship between people and the context in which leadership is enacted, we need to be aware not to succumb to overemphasize attributes of leader as a person. The relative importance of the situation or context in which a leader is operating needs to be recognized (Schrujjer&Vasina, 2002).

Exhibit 1: Tips for Training

Source of Efficacy	Key for Successful Training and Transfer to the job	Training Recommendations
1. Mastery experience and performance attainment	Trainees must learn they are the cause of their performance.	1. Plenty of practice so mastery (as defined by the training objective) is reached. 2. Break learning into series of obtainable endpoints to help self-confirmation of skills. 3. Provide feedback on progress (not shortfalls) and contributions.
2. Vicarious experience and modeling	Model(s) used should have similar demographic attributes, and the training being done should be similar to what the trainees will be doing back on the job.	1. Carefully select models used in the training to have similar characteristics. 2. Set up training so that trainees perceive performance is due to capability of the model and not other factors. 3. Models should take diagnostic perspective (i.e., focus on test and if mistake is made interpret as way to learn rather than personal inadequacy).

3. Social persuasion	All comments have impact, so feedback must be phrased positively to build trainee confidence.	1. Set trainees up for success so feedback comments can be very positive. 2. Trainer must be careful and sensitive to keep positive things that are said and done in the presence of the trainee.
4. Physical and psychological arousal	Make sure trainees experiencing physical or psychological symptoms interpret them as the nature of the training task and not some personal inadequacy (i.e. lack of ability).	1. Trainees must understand that the need to exert considerable physical (or psychological) effort does not mean a lack of personal capability. 2. Getting trainees physically and psychologically fit may help arouse motivation to learn and be successful.

Chapter 3

Promoting Optimism

Optimism has surfaced as a major component of the recent positive psychological movement. However, it has long been recognized by both psychologists and people in general. The positive impact of optimism on physical and psychological health is well documented. It is accepted that the impact is manifest in terms of academic, athletic, political and occupational success. At the same time, pessimism is known to lead to passivity, failure, social estrangement, depression and mortality.

In defining optimism, contemporary psychologists go far beyond the old adage of the "power of positive thinking". Psychology treats optimism as a cognitive characteristic in terms of a generalized positive outcome expectancy. Seligman (1990) defines it positive casual attribution (explanatory style). Optimism is also often used in relation to other positive constructs such as emotional intelligence. Emotional intelligence expert Daniel Goleman devotes considerable attention to the role of optimism in his discussion of emotional intelligence. University of Michigan psychologist Christopher Peterson points out: Optimism is not simply cold cognition, and if we forget the emotional flavor that pervades optimism, we can make little sense of the fact that optimism is both motivated and motivating".

Nature of Optimism

In the past, many classical authors such as Freud and Erikson viewed optimism as a bias in human nature. According to them, healthy individuals need to make objective and appropriate estimates of their realities. Optimism, from this perspective, is a kind of illusion.

However more recently, psychologists have viewed this bias as a kind of creative illusion. More in tune with mainstream modern psychology is to treat optimism as an individual difference. People have varying degrees of optimism. It focuses on cognitively determined expectation and casual attributions.

Seligman in particular is associated with the attributional approach. He uses the term *explanatory style* to depict how an individual habitually attributes the causes of failure, misfortune or bad events.

Here are the causal attributions or explanatory styles pessimists and optimists tend to habitually use in interpreting personal bad events.

1. Pessimists make *internal* (their own fault), *stable* (will last a long time), and *global* (will undermine everything they do) attribution.
2. *Optimists* make *external* (not their fault), *unstable* (temporary setback), and *specific* (problem only in this situation) attribution.

Research continues on explanatory style. It is found that the internality attribution does not hold up as well as stability or globality. Overall, optimism is linked with desirable characteristics such as happiness, perseverance, achievement and health.

Optimism in Workplace

Optimism could be very positive force in workplace. Optimism may be motivated to work harder, be more satisfied and have high morale, have high levels of aspiration and set strech goals, persevere in the face of obstacles. The "half-empty, half-full" example gives some real world scenarios of pessimistic and optimistic people. There are some jobs and career fields where optimism is especially valuable (e.g., sale, advertising, public relation, product design, customer service, health and social service)

Seligman carried out a major project of Metropolitan Life Insurance (USA). He measured optimism with the use of his instruments "Attributional Style Questionnaire (ASQ)". Results showed that agents who scored in the most optimistic half of the ASQ had sold 37 percent more insurance on average in their first two years than agents who scored in the pessimistic half. Agents who scored in the top 10 percent sold 88 percent more than the most pessimistic 10 percent.

Apart from the comprehensive Met Life Study, other studies have examined competent managers and found that they attribute their failures to correctable mistakes and then they persevere. A recent field study found positive association between optimism of military cadets and their leadership potential. Another study of business leaders found that on average they were more optimistic than a sample of non-leaders.

Training for Optimism

A fundamental issue in the context of optimism concerns the question of its trainability. Some researchers view it as dispositional – a trait like concept. On the contrary Seligman has popularized of the construct of learned optimism.

According to Seligman (1990), optimism can be included by implementing ABCDE model. According to him, the phenomenon starts with an activating event or antecedent (A). This event generates some belief (B) which, in turn, leads to a consequence (C). For example, a teacher may experience an unpleasant situation (some students creating chaos) in the class. This may lead to the belief that the teacher is incompetent. This belief, in turn may induce a consequence of depression.

However, Seligman suggests that individual needs to adopt a remediation method – disputation (D). He or she may argue that only a small number of students are showing signs of indiscipline. Alternatively, he or she may think to meet his or her colleagues collectively to find out what is happening in their classes. The disputation would be instrumental in dispelling his or her faulty thought. In addition to this method of restructuring thought, the individual would benefit by adopting activity – energization (E). He or she may try to meet colleagues to discuss and find solutions. Thus depressive cycle of ABC is broken by adopting D (disputation) and E (Energization). Thus, optimism can be trained.

Finally, it must be remembered that extreme optimism may lead to meaningless or dysfunctional outcomes. Optimistically driven behaviour may be aimed at pointless pursuits (I would finish in the top five) or unrealistic goals. Thus, realistic optimism results in more effective leadership than false optimism. Thus, with appropriate bounds, realistic optimism (or dynamic optimism is functional optimism) is a valuable resource.

Chapter 4

Fostering Resilience

The capacity to minimize and prevent the negative effects of adverse circumstances is an attribute with special significance. In the past, people were talking about 3RS (reading, writing and arithmetic) to denote essential qualities. Today, we also stress 3RS signifying reasoning, responsibility and resilience.

Since circumstances are changing very fast, the ability to dynamically reinvent activity models has become the imperative. Resilience is not just about responding to a setback. It is about continually anticipating and adjusting to deep trends that can impair progress. It's about having the capacity to change even before the cause for change becomes obvious.

Theories abound about what produces resilience, but three fundamental characteristic seem to set resilient people and organizations apart from others. One or two of these qualities make it possible to bounce back from hardship, but true resilience requires all three.

Features of Resilience

The first characteristic is the capacity to accept and face down reality. In looking hard at reality, we prepare ourselves to act in ways that allow us to endure and survive hardship. A common belief about resilience is that it stems from an optimistic nature. That's true but only as long as such optimism does not distort our sense of reality. In extremely adverse situations, rose-coloured thinking can actually spell disaster.

Prior to September 11, 2001, Morgan Stanley, the famous investment bank, was the largest tenant in the World Trade Centre (U.S.A.). The company had some 2,700 employees working in the south tower on 22 floors between the 43rd and the 74th. On that horrible day, the first plane hit the north tower at 8:46 A.M, and Morgan Stanley started evacuating just one minute later. When the second plane crashed into the south tower 15 minutes after that, Morgan Stanley's offices were largely empty. The company lost only seven people despite receiving an almost direct hit.

Of course, the organization was plain lucky to be in the second tower. The offices in the first attack could not have done anything to save its employees. Yes, it was Morgan Stanley's hard-nose realism that enabled the company to benefit from its luck. Soon after the 1993 attack on the World Trade Centre, service management anticipated its vulnerability.

The ability to see reality is closely linked to the second building block of resilience, the propensity to make meaning of terrible times. Generally, people under stress throw up their hands and cry, "How can this be happening to me". But resilient people devise constructs about their suffering to create some sort of meaning for themselves and others.

The concept was beautifully articulated by Viktor Frankl, an Austrian psychiatrist and Auschwitz survivor. In the midst of staggering suffering, Frankl invented meaning therapy, a humanistic therapy technique that helps individuals make the kinds of decisions that will create significance in their lives.

In his book Man's Search for Meaning, Frankl described the pivotal moment in the camp when he developed meaning therapy. He was on his way to work one day, worrying whether he should trade his last cigarette for a bowl of soup. He wondered how he was going to work with a new foreman whom he knew to be particularly sadistic. Suddenly, he was disgusted by just how trivial and meaningless his life had become. He realized that to survive, he had to find some purpose. Frankl did so by imagining himself giving a lecture after the war on the psychology, of the concentration camp, to help outsiders understand what he had been through. Although he was not sure that he would survive Frankl created some concrete goals for himself. In doing so, he succeeded in rising above the sufferings of the moment. As he put in his book; "We must never forget that we may also find meaning in life even when confronted with a hopeless situation when facing a fate that cannot be changed".

Since finding meaning in one's environment is such an important aspect of resilience, it should come as no surprise that the most successful organizations and people possess strong value system. Strong values infuse an environment with meaning because they offer ways to interpret and shape events. While it's popular these days to ridicule values, it's surely no coincidence that the most resilient organization in the world has been the religious institutions.

The third building block of resilience is the ability to make do with whatever is at hand. Psychologists follow the lead of French anthropologist Levi Strauss in calling this skill bricolage. The roots of that word are closely tied to the concert of resilience. It literally means "bouncing back". Levi Strauss write; "In its old sense, the verb bricoler --- was always used with reference to some extraneous movement; a ball rebounding, a dog straying, or a horse swerving from its direct course to avoid an obstacle".

Bricolage in the modern sense can be defined as a kind of inventiveness, an ability to improvise a solution to a problem without proper or obvious tools or materials. In the concentration camps, for example, resilient inmates knew to pocket pieces of string or wire whenever they found them. The string or wire might later become useful to fix a pair of shoes perhaps, which in freezing conditions might make the difference between life and death.

Resilience is a way of facing and understanding the world. Resilient people and organizations face reality with staunchness, make meaning of hardship instead of crying out in despair and improvise solutions from air. Others do not. This is the nature of resilience.

Training of Resilience

The findings on resilience suggest that the greatest threats to individuals are those adversities that undermine the basic human protective system for development. It follows that efforts to promote competence and resilience should focus on strategies that prevent damage to restore or compensate for threats to these basic system. Resilience models suggest that programs will be most effective when they tap into powerful adaptation of system. One example is provided by the mastery motivational system. Masten suggest three basic strategies for intervention.

Risk Focused Strategy. This strategyaims to reduce the exposure to hazardous experiences. Examples of risk-focused strategies include care to prevent accident hazards, education reforms to reduce the stressfulness or community efforts to reduce homelessness. Here the interest is to remove or reduce threat exposure.

Asset-Focused Strategies. Here approaches aim to increase the amount of access to or quality of resources individual's need for the development of competence. Examples of resources that are assumed to have direct effect are providing a mentor (tutor) or building a recreation center with programs. Other assets are assumed to operate indirectly through strengthening the social or financial capital of the individual. Examples include the establishment of resource centres, career counseling centers and similar avenues. These are directed at asset-building strategy.

Process-Focused Strategies. The strategies aim to mobilize the fundamental protective system. In this case, efforts go beyond simply removing risks or adding assets, but instead attempt to influence *processes* that will change an individual's life. Example include programs designed to improve the quality of relationship and efforts to activate the mastery motivation system through a sequence of graduated mastery experiences that enable an individual to experience success and build self-efficacy and motivation to succeed in life.

In effect, these programs aim to prevent or reduce problems in development by promoting good adaptation. Each has a different emphasis, yet they all utilize multiple strategies to reduce risks and increase protection in life.

Chapter 5

Emotional Intelligence

Intelligence is a universal term which refers to all forms of man's complex mental activities. It refers to the ability to understand, act, interpret, and predict the future, and to achieve and handle relationships, information, concepts and abstract symbols. Intelligence is thus a commonly used word to express universal capacity required for survival and progress beyond the present.

Rational Intelligence

Intelligence is a process of cognition. Cognition refers to the ways people acquire, store, retrieve, and use information. All the fundamental psychological processes such as learning, perception, memory, concept formation, thinking, reasoning, problem solving, decision making and creativity are related to intelligence. Therefore, intelligent behaviour includes all forms of cognitive behaviour such as attending, perceiving, learning, memorizing, thinking and predicting. Intelligence is an abstract concept. It can not be observed directly. It can only be estimated on the basis of individual's performance on tests and real life situations.

Sternberg (1905) has given us the famous triarchic theory or intelligence. The theory offers three faces of intelligence for ease of understanding of the important construct of intelligence. The first face involves the cognitive mechanisms of the mind which explains our ability to produce more or less intelligent behaviour. The second face comprises of the essential characteristic of learning – how to do things and actually doing the things. This part of the theory is primarily concerned with the way individuals deal with novel tasks and develop automatic, routine responses for well-practiced tasks. The third face of the theory relates to intelligence that involves the external world. This refers to the way people adapt to select, and shape their environment. Such behaviours are essential in managing the day-to-day business functions in an organization.

Sternberg proposes three different components: 1) meta components, which are used in planning, adopting strategies, and evaluating one's performance of a task; 2) performance components which include cognitive processes that are used in performing a task; and 3) knowledge acquisition components, or which are concerned with how we learn concepts, techniques, processes through formal instructions or acquired spontaneously through experience.

Gardner (1983, 1993, 2001, 2002, 2006) has proposed eight types or intelligence. They are described in the following list along with examples of the occupations in which they are reflected as strengths (Campbell, Campbell, &Dickinson, 2004).

- *Verbal Skill:* The ability to think in words and use language to express meaning
  Occupations: Authors, journalists, speakers
- *Mathematical Skills:* The ability to carry out mathematical operations
  Occupation: Scientists, engineers, accountants
- *Spatial Skills:* The ability to think three-dimensionally

Occupation: Architects, artists, sailors
- *Bodily-Kinesthetic* Skills: The ability to manipulate objects and be physically adept
Occupations: Surgeons, craftspeople, dancers, athletes
- *Musical Skills:* A sensitivity to pitch, melody, rhythm, and tone
Occupation: Composers, musicians, and sensitive listeners
- *Interpersonal Skills:* The ability to understand and effectively interact with others
Occupation: Successful teachers, mental health professionals
- *Interpersonal Skill:* The ability to understand oneself
Occupations: Theologians, Psychologists
- *Naturalist Skills:* The ability to observe patterns in nature and understand nature and human-made systems
Occupations: Farmers, botanists, ecologists, landscapers

According to Gardner, everyone has all of the preceding intelligences but to varying degrees. As a result, we prefer to learn and process information in different ways. People learn best when they can apply their strong intelligence to the task.

Both Gardner's and Stenberg's theories include one or more categories related to social intelligence. In Gardner's theory, the categories are interpersonal intelligence and intrapersonal intelligence; in Sternberg's theory, practical intelligence. Another theory that emphasizes interpersonal, intrapersonal and practical aspects of intelligence is called **emotional intelligence,** which has been popularized by Daniel Goleman (1995) in his book *Emotional Intelligence.* The concept of emotional intelligence was initially developed by Peter Salovey and John Mayer (1990), who define it as the ability to perceive and express emotion accurately and adaptively (such as taking the perspective of others), to understand emotion and emotional knowledge (such as understanding the role that emotions play in friendship and marriage), to use feelings to facilitate thought (such as being in a positive mood, which is linked to creative thinking), and to manage emotion in oneself and others (such as being able to control one's anger).

Evolution of the Construct

Recently, the Mayer-Salovey-Caruso Emotional intelligence Test (MSCEIT) was developed to measure the four aspects of emotional intelligence just described Perceiving emotions, understanding emotions, facilitating thought, and managing emotions (Mayer, Salovey, & Caruso, 2002). The test consists of 141 items, can be given to individuals 17 years of age and older, and takes about 30-45 minutes to administer. Because the MSCEIT has only been available since 2001, few studies have been conducted to examine its ability to predict outcomes (Salovey & Pizarro, 2003). One recent study that used the MSCEIT found that youths with higher emotional intelligence were less likely to have smoked cigarettes or to have used alcohol (Trinidad & Johnson 2002).

Stenberg	Gardner	Mayer/Salovey/Goleman
Analytical	Verbal, Mathematical	
Creative	Spatial, Movement, Musical	
Practical	Impersonal, Intra-personal, Naturalistic	Emotional

Emotion is experienced in life as well as work. Though behavioural scientists have studied emotion in great detail, its immense role in the study of work and leadership is of recent origin, Daniel Goleman et al. (2001) have observed that the emotional impact of a leader is almost never discussed in the workplace or in the literature on leadership and performance. The reason for this has been suggested by Steve Fineman (1996) as follows:

> Deeply rooted in Western (especially male) cultural beliefs about the expression of emotion is the belief that organizational order/worker efficiency are matters of the rational, that is non-emotional, activity. Cool strategic thinking is not to be sullied by messy feelings. Efficient thought and behaviour tame emotion. Accordingly good organizations are places where feelings are managed, designed out, or removed.

Guy Lubitsh and John Higgins (2001) have observed that ignoring emotions could lead to tragic consequences. They have cited the classic example ofChallenger disaster in this context. They say that the engineers aboard the space shuttle did not volunteer to transmit information when the shuttle developed a serious snag to the management. As employees they were very much aware of the bullying that they would receive if any opposing or unpopular line of thought was passed on to the management. This perceived unwillingness on the part of top management, known in current leadership literature as leadership failure, led to the disastrous end of mission Challenger in space research. Peter Frost (2003) has described the emotionally insensitive attitudes and behaviours of managers as highly toxic and debilitating. He has prescribed empathetic listening by managers to the views and suggestions of employees as a definite tactic to cleanse the emotional toxins in organizations. Kjell Nordstrom (2000) has emphasized the urgent need in today's excess economy for feeling as well as thinking people. He says organizational success comes from attracting the emotional consumer *or* colleague, not the rational one. The need of the hour is not only agile thinkers, but acting, feeling and communicating human beings as well. Excitement is contagious: it can stimulate others into action (Hatfield et al., 1992). Expression of positive emotions has extremely positive outcomes. When people witness acts of moral beauty – a young person helping an elderly woman cleaning her driveway, a social worker ministering to the poor – they experience a distinct emotion (called) elevation – an emotion that involves a physical feeling, typically to the chest, and motivates people to want to help others (Carpenter, 2001). Goleman et al. (2001) have observed that when the leader is in a happy mood, the people around him view everything in a more positive light. That, in turn, makes them optimistic about achieving their goals, enhances their creativity and the efficiency of their decision making, and predisposes them to be helpful. Ostell (1996) has observed that emotional reactions may adversely affect one's judgment, task performance, well-being and interpersonal relationships. Kevin Daniels (1999) says that negative emotions may affect the manager's strategic decision making function in an organization. Self-control under pressure is often regarded as a major attribute ofeffective leaders. Emotions are often seen as the basis ofirrational decisions in organization. Strong negative emotions causing adverse consequences often lead to great organizational costs (Lubitsh and Higgins, 2001).

The emotional mind is often quicker than the rational mind. It acts without considering what it is doing. This implies that emotion has a more immediate and perhaps even greater impact on our behaviour than rational thought However, it is difficult and even unrealistic to separate feeling from thinking. The 'emotional brain' is located in the limbic system called amygdala. It works very closely and speedily with the 'thinking brain' located in the prefrontal cortex. This relationship provides us with what we call 'emotional intelligence' (Goleman, 1998a). Effective learning depends on the interaction between cognitive and emotional processes.

We've all heard of IQ. And at one time or another most of us have met someone who's technically smart, even brilliant, but otherwise not very bright. They aren't successful at work, they can't seem to keep relationships, or know how to make themselves happy. That's probably because they have a high IQ but rank low on the emotional intelligence scale. Similarly, we all know people who without a university education, shine both at work and at home. As Daniel Goleman points out in his national best seller "Emotional Intelligence" a high IQ doesn't necessarily predict who will succeed in life. Psychologists agree that IQ contributes only about 20 per cent to what determines success. The rest. comes from what Goleman calls emotional intelligence. Emotions have been talked about and researched for years. The phrase "emotional intelligence" was coined years ago by Yale psychologist Peter Salovey and University of New Hampshire professor John Mayer. Emotional intelligence, or rather EQ, describes qualities in a person such as self-awareness, self-motivation, impulse control and empathy. In essence, emotional intelligence means being smart about our emotions. It is not the opposite of IQ, it is just different.

IQ vs EQ
EI refers to the capacity for recognizing our own feelings and

those of others, for motivating ourselves, and for managing *emotions in* us and in our relationships. EI describes abilities distinct from, but complementary to, academic intelligence or the purely cognitive capacities measured by IQ. Traditionally, the emphasis when evaluating potential performance has been on intellectual; now compelling research indicates that emotional intelligence is twice as important as IQ plus technical skill for outstanding performance. When IQ test scores are correlated with how well people perform in their careers, the highest estimate of how much difference IQ accounts for is about 25%. As a manager of a telecommunications company sums it up, "You don't compete with products alone anymore, but how well you use your people".

An emotional competence is a learned capacity based on emotional intelligence that results in outstanding performance at work. For superior performance in jobs of all kinds, emotional competence matters twice as much as IQ plus technical skill combined.

What is Emotional Intelligence?

'Emotional intelligence is the capacity of recognizing our own feeling and those of others, for motivating ourselves, for managing emotions well in ourselves and in our relationships. Behaviourists have identified a set of competencies that differentiate individuals and groups with Emotional Intelligence. The competencies fall into four clusters:

Self-awareness: Capacity for understanding one's emotions, one's strengths, and one' weaknesses.

Self-management: Capacity for effectively managing one's motives and regulating one's behaviour in-groups and in teams.

Social Awareness: Capacity for understanding what others are saying and feeling and why they feel and act as they do.

Social Skills: Capacity for acting in such a way that one is able to get desired results from others and reach personal goals.

Significance of EI

There are compelling reasons as to why emotional intelligence (EI) is seminal in our scheme of life. From evolutionary stand-point, EI is more important than rational intelligence. When living beings were in the process of evolution and the stage of reptiles was attained, some ring-like structures began to form near the brain-stem (the region connecting the brain and the spinal cord). Since "limbus" is the Greek word for "ring", the structures were called *limbic system*. The limbic system- took care of emotion. In other words, the *feeling brain* came first. Subsequently the thinking centers in the brain (cortex) were formed. Since smell sensation was important from survival point of view, nose center came first. Thus, *feeling brain is older than the thinking brain*. It is also observed that the brain is structurally one, but functionally two. The left hemisphere of the brain is concerned with language and logical functions. The right brain is mostly linked with emotion and pattern recognition. The dissection of the human brain reveals that the left hemisphere is slightly bigger than the right one. It is indicative of the fact that human beings use more of, logical thinking and reasoning than positive emotion. It is asserted that this is indicative of lopsided development. The situation has to be rectified and humans need to balance the activities of the left and the right hemispheres.

Chapter 6

Stimulating Hope

In all of human history, there has been a need to believe that bad could be transformed into good, that ugly could become beautiful, and that problems could be solved. But people differ in the degree to which they view such changes as possible.

Parameters of Hope

Hope denotes goal-directed thinking in which the person utilizes *pathways* thinking (the perceived capacity to find routes to desired goals) and *agency* thinking (the requisite motivation to use the routes).

Goals can vary temporally-from those that will be reacted in the next few minutes (short-term goals) to those that will take months or even years to reach (long-term). Likewise, the goals may be approach oriented (aimed at reaching a desired goal) or preventive (aimed at stopping an undesirable goal). Lastly, goals can vary in relation to the difficulty of attainment, with some goals quite easy and others quite difficult.

Pathways thinking have been shown to relate to the production of alternative routes when original ones are blocked, as has positive self-talk about finding routes to desired goals ("I will find a way to solve this"). Similarly, people having greater capacity for agency thinking also endorse energetic personal self-talk ("I will keep going").

High hopers have positive emotional sets and a sense of zest that stems from their histories of success in past pursuits, whereas low hopers have negative emotional sets and a sense of emotional flatness that stems from their past histories of having failed in goal pursuits.

The person may encounter a stressor that potentially blocks the actual goal pursuit. Hope theory proposes that the successful pursuit of desired goal, especially when circumventing stressful impediments, results in positive emotions and continued goal pursuit efforts. On the other hand if a person's goal pursuit is not successful, then negative emotion should result, and the goal pursuit process should be undermined.

Furthermore, such a stressor is interpreted differentially depending on the person's overall level of hope. High hopers construe such barriers as challenges and will explore alternative routes and apply their motivations to those routes. Typically having experienced success in working around such blockages, the high hopes are propelled onward by their positive emotions. The low hopers, however, become stuck because they cannot find alternate routes; in turn, their negative emotions and ruminations stymie their goal pursuits.

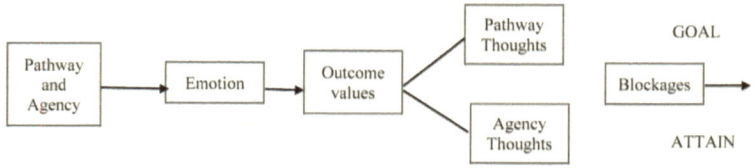

Antecedents of Hope

Hope is a learned cognitive set about goal-directed thinking. The teaching of pathways and agency is an inherent part of parenting, and the components of hopeful thoughts are in place by age two. Pathways thinking reflects basic cause-and-effect learning that the child acquires from thinking, with the latter being posited to begin around age one. Agency thought reflects the baby's increasing insight as to the fact that she is the causal force in many of the cause-and-effect sequences in her surrounding environment.

Snyder (2000) has proposed that strong attachment to caregivers in crucial for imparting hope. Traumatic events across the course of childhood also have been linked to the lessoning of hope and there has been research support for the negative impact of some of these traumas.

What Hope Predicts

In general, Hope Scale scores have predicted outcomes in academics, sports, physical health, adjustment and well-being. For example, in the area of academics, higher Hope Scale scores taken at the beginning of college have predicted better cumulative grade point averages. In the area of sports, high Hope Scale scores taken at the beginning of college track season have predicted the superior performance of male athletes and have done so beyond the coach's rating of natural athletic abilities. In the area of adjustment, higher Hope Scale scores have related to various indices of elevated happiness, satisfaction, positive emotions, and getting along with others.

Hope researchers have expanded their construct to explore what is called **collective hope.** Collective hope reflects the level of goal-directed thinking of a large group of people. Often, such collective hope is operative when several people join together to tackle a goal that would be impossible for any one person. The notion of collective hope has relevance for the topics of environmental protection and poverty alleviation.

Chapter 7

Flow

Viktor Frankl, the Austrian psychologist and psychiatrist who survived the worst Nazi concentration camp, once remarked: "Don't aim at success – the more you aim at it and make it a target, the more you are going to miss it". This is also true of happiness. Considered from this angle, the title "seeking happiness" is a faulty rubric. Happiness cannot be pursued; it must ensue as the unintended side-effect of one's personal dedication to a cause greater than oneself.

Books cannot give recipes for how to be happy. Optimal experience depends on the ability to control what happens in consciousness moment to moment. Each individual has to achieve it on the basis of his/her own individual effort and creativity.

The leading psychologist Mihaly Csikszentmihalyi (pronounced as ME-high CHICK-sent-mehigh-ee) popularized the concept.

The Optimal Experience: Basic Considerations
In order to maximize the possibility of optimal experience, we have to consider some basic ingredients.

The roots of discontents. The universe is not hostile, nor it is friendly. It is simply indifferent. Whether we are happy does not depend on the controls we are able to exert over the forces of the universe. Certainly we should keep on learning how to master the external environment, because our physical survival may depend on it. But such mastery is not going to add a jot to how good we as individuals feel, or reduce the chaos of the world as we experience it. To do that we must learn to achieve mastery over consciousness.

Evidence suggests that most people are caught up on this frustrating treadmill of rising expectations. However, some individuals have found ways to escape it. These are people who regardless of their material conditions have been able to improve the quality of their lives. The greatest strength of them is that they are in control of their lives.

The path of libering oneself from the slavery of external conditioning – the control of life – is the control of consciousness. The control of life and control of consciousness are synonymous. But control over consciousness is not simply a cognitive skill. It requires the commitment of emotion and will. It is not enough to *know* how to do it; one must do it consistently, in the same way as musicians keep practicing.

The anatomy of consciousness. In the past, people who could control their thoughts and feelings were considered to be the right kind of individuals. It is not so now. Yet despite the dictates of fashions, those who gain control over consciousness are happy people.

To achieve such mastery over consciousness, one has to understand it. Like any other dimension of human behaviour, it is the result of biological process. It exists only because of the incredibly complex architecture if our nervous system, which in its turn, is built up according to instructions contained in the protein molecules of our chromosomes. At the same time, the way in which consciousness works is not entirely controlled by its biological programming; it is self-directed.

A phenomenological view of consciousness based on information theory posits **consciousness as intentionally ordered information.** The intentions we either inherit or acquire are organized in hierarchies of goals. The hierarchy specifies the order of perception. For example, achieving a change is more important for a social activist. Most people adopt sensible goals based on the needs of their bodies (to be healthy, to lead a comfortably life). But individuals who depart from norms – saints, poets, philosophers – look for different things.

Consciousness can be ordered in terms of different goals and intentions. Each of us has this freedom to control our subjective reality.

While controlling consciousness, the limits of consciousness must not be lost sight of. In average, 185 billion events are to be enjoyed over our mortal days of seventy years. The information *we allow* into *consciousness* is very important; it determines the quality of our lives.

Attention is a psychic energy which determines what will or will not appear in consciousness. When information that keeps coming to the consciousness is congruent with goals, psychic energy flows effortlessly. There is no need to worry.

There are situations in which *attention* can be freely invested to achieve a person's goals, because there is no desire to defend against. This state is called **flow experience**. When a person is able to organize his or her consciousness so as to experience flow as often as possible, the quality of life is inevitably going to improve.

Pleasure versus quality experience. Pleasure is an important component of the quality of life, but by itself does not bring happiness. Sleep, rest and food provides *restorative happiness* – homeostatic experience that return consciousness to order after the needs of the body are fulfilled. Yet they do not provide psychological growth. They do not add complexity to the self. Pleasure helps to maintain order, by itself cannot create new order in consciousness.

The quality experience (optimal experience) is occasioned by flow.

Flow Experience

Occasionally flow may occur by chance, because of a fortunate coincidence of external and internal conditions. While such events may happen occasionally, it is much more likely that flow will result either from structured activity, or from an individual's ability to make flow occur, or both.

Flow features. Irrespective of activities (dance, writing, yoga, chess playing) flow experience has *eight* features.

1. Experience occurs when we have chance of completing.
2. Must be able to concentrate on what we are doing.
3. Task has clear goals.
4. Task provides feedback.
5. Deep yet effortless involvement (Away from worries and frustrations)
6. Allows individuals to exercise sense of control.
7. The self disappears in the beginning, but self appears stronger after flow experience is over
8. Sense of duration of time is altered.

As indicated, flow denotes the merging of action and awareness. *Person's attention is completely absorbed by the activity.*

A dancer comments: "My concentration is complete.

My mind is not wondering, I am not thinking something else; I am totally involved in what I am doing. My energy is flowing very smoothly. I feel relaxed, comfortable, and energetic". A writer comments: "The act of writing justifies poetry. The purpose of the flow is to keep on flowing, not looking for a peak or utopia but staying in flow. It is not a moving up but a continuous flowing; you move up to keep the flow going".

The Contours of Flow

Flow occurs when there is a great deal of match between high levels of perceived skill and high degree of challenge in the task. The situation can be depicted schematically.

	Perceived Ability	
Level of Challenge in Task	Low	High
High	Anxiety	Flow
Low	Apathy	Boredom

However, there is a broad range of activity which offers flow potentials.

The body in flow. Everything the body does is enjoyable. When left undeveloped, the senses give us chaotic information. An untrained body moves in random and clumsy way, an insensitive eye presents ugly or uninteresting sights, the unmusical ear hears furring noises. If the functions of the body are left to atrophy, the quality of life becomes merely adequate. But if one takes control of what the body can do, entropy yields to a sense of enjoyable harmony. The human body is capable of hundreds of separate functions: seeing, hearing, touching, running, swimming, throwing, catching, climbing. It should be stressed that body does not produce flow merely by its movements. The mind is involved as well. To get enjoyment from swimming, one needs to cultivate a set of appropriate skills. However, skills require the concentration of attention. Without the relevant thought, motive, and feeling, it would be impossible to enjoy swimming.

The flow of thoughts. The famous French philosopher and essayist Bacon made a remark four hundred years ago: "Reflection is the purest form of pleasure". To enjoy a mental activity, one must meet the same conditions that make physical activities enjoyable. There must be skill in a symbolic domain; there have to be rules, a goal and a way of obtaining feedback. One must be able to concentrate and interact with opportunities at a level commensurate with one's skills.

When left alone, with no demand on attention, the basic disorder of mind reveals Mind follows random pattern. To avoid this condition, people fill their mind with whatever information is available (i.e., television).

In reviewing conditions that help to establish order in mind, the important role of memory has to be recognized, followed by discussion on history, science, and philosophy.

The first step is to learn what others have thought about the matter. By reading, listening and talking selectively one can form of an idea of what the "state of the art" is in the field is. Then there comes a point where a person is ready to pass from the status of passive consumer to that of active producer.

Work as flow. When asked for his recipe for happiness, Sigmund Freud gave a simple answer: "work and love". It is true that if one finds flow in work and in relation with other people, one is well on the way towards improving the quality of life as a whole.

The more a job inherently resembles a game with variety, appropriate and flexible challenge, clear goals, immediate feedback – the more enjoyable it will be regardless of the worker's level of development.

Hunting is a good example of this kind. Many people are still doing it as a form of hobby. Same is true of fishing. Compared to hunting and herding, firming is difficult to enjoy.

In theory, any job could be a source of flow. For example, surgery is found to be flow-producing for some and routine matters for others.

To improve the quality of life through work, two complementary strategies are needed. On the one hand, jobs should be redesigned so that they resemble as closely as possible flow activities – as do hunting, cottage weaving and surgery. But it will also be necessary to help people develop *autotelic personalities* by training them to recognize opportunities for actions, to hone their skills to set reasonable goals. Any one of these strategies won't bring flow; the combination is needed.

Enjoying solitude and other people. In addition to work, social bonding also offers flow experience. Whether we are in the company of others or not makes a great difference to the quality of experience. We are biologically programmed to find other human beings the most important objects in the world. Because they can make life either very interesting or utterly miserable, how to manage relationship with them makes great difference to our happiness. If we learn to make our relation with others more like flow experience, our quality of life as a whole is going to be much more improved.

On the other hand, we also value privacy and often wish to be left alone. Yet it frequently turns out as soon as we are alone, we begin to feel depressed.

There is no question that, we are programmed to seek out the company of others. At the same time there is a long tradition of longing solitude. It is not difficult to reconcile. A person can make profitable use of both.

Most people feel a nearly intolerable sense of emptiness when they are alone. Most usual ways of coping with the dread solitude include TV watching, drugs and sex. They focus attention naturally. In so doing they exclude unwanted contents from the mind. What they fail to do is to develop any of the attentional habit that might lend to a greater complexity of consciousness.

The ultimate test for the ability to control the quality of experience is what a person does in solitude, with no external demands to give structure to attention. Learning to use tike alone, instead of escaping from it, is especially important in our early years. To fill free time with activities that require concentration, that increase skills, that lead to the development of the self, is not the same as killing time by watching television or taking recreational drugs.

Support Systems

Some individuals have immense capabilities to generate flow for themselves. However, socio-cultural systems, communities, families and other networks also have resources to enhance flow experience for its people.

Many cultures provide various rituals, dance-forms and other flow-generating activities. Similarly, families may induce flows through their goals. Extrinsic needs are not sufficient. Some of the goals may be greater and long-term. Such goals provide differentiation and integration. **Differentiation** means each person is encouraged to develop his or her interest, maximize personal skills and fulfill individual goals. **Integration** guarantees that all members pay attention to help and cheer up others.

Chapter 8

Work–Life Integration

Over the past decades the issues of work-family and work-life balances have received extensive attention. Concerns about work-life balance have become salient for a number of reasons. Demographic and social changes have resulted in more women entering the workforce. Working mothers now constitute the norm rather than the exceptions. Technological advances (e.g., cell phones, e-mail, fax) have made it easier for work demands to intrude into family and personal life. Moreover, the global competition has increased pressures on individuals and organizations to become more flexible and responsive to change.

A blurring of boundaries between work and home life and an increasing difficulty in maintaining a balance between these two domains is now recognized. Frequently this issue is seen a difficulty in maintaining *'work-family balance'*. However, it is also important to recognize that people are involved in multiple roles outside their family life. These roles may include leisure roles, community roles and religious roles. The term *'work-life balance'* is thus seen as more inclusive. There is also a tendency to use *'work-life integration'* on the rationale that a balance implying 50:50 investment or allocation may not be a desired situation for many people.

Conceptual Frameworks

In order to understand work-family balance (or work-life integration), a number of conceptual models have been advanced. Some models evolved in the course of past research whereas other perspectives are of recent development.

Dominant Models

Through the 1980s and the 1990s the amount of research on work and family roles increased considerably. The proliferation of research led to several models depicting the relationship between work and family roles. Edwards and Rothbard (2000) provide a review of existing research. They identify six models: spillover, compensation, segmentation, resource-drain, congruence, and work-family conflict.

Spillover. Spillover is a process whereby experience in one role affect experiences in the other, rendering the roles more similar. Research has examined the spillover of mood, values, skills and behaviours from one role to another, although the majority has focused on moods. The spillover model is supported when there is a significant positive relationship between measures of work non-work experiences. Spillover can take two forms. The first one is the similarity between a work construct and a related construct in the non-work role. For example, a person who is highly satisfied with his or her work organization becomes highly satisfied with his or her experiences in the family role. The second form of spillover entails the transference of experience intact between work and non-work domains. For instance, fatigue from work is transmitted and there is display of fatigue in home. Researchers generally use Experience Sampling Methodology (ESM) to document spillover. People are asked to describe some aspect of their work and non-work domain separately. Later, analysis is geared to find out the intensity of correspondence between the two. The high degree of similarity attests to the level of spillover.

Compensation. Compensation refers to a relationship between work and non-work roles whereby people attempt to make up for deficiency in one role through greater involvement in other role. It entails a negative relationship between constructs in the two roles. Persons can compensate for dissatisfaction in role in a number of ways. They can reduce the importance attached to the less rewarding role or they can seek rewards and invest more efforts in an alternative role. A number of studies find that managers experiencing disappointment in their work seek fulfillment in their family lives. More recently, Rothbard (2001) found that women who experienced negative affect from family were more engaged with their work.

Segmentation. Unlike the spillover and compensation models, the segmentation model posits no systematic relationship between work and non-work roles. Instead, segmentation has been used to describe the separation of work and family, such that the two roles do not influence one another. Initially, segmentation was viewed as the natural division of work and family due to the physical and temporal separation of the two roles and to their innately different functions. However, segmentation has been recently conceptualized as an active psychological process whereby people may choose to maintain a boundary between work and family. For example, some people may actively suppress work-related thoughts, feelings and behaviours while at home, and vice versa. From this perspective, segmentation may be a strategy for work family *boundary management*. This may be helpful for keeping work and non-work domains separate and maintaining an impermeable boundary between work and non-work roles.

Conflict. Role conflict is a central concern to work-family researchers. Borrowing from the role theory tradition, classic conceptualization of conflict model suggests that an individual encounters role conflict when the demands and expectations from one role interfere with the individual's ability to meet demands and expectations from another role. An example of role conflict is that of an employee who is simultaneously pressured to work overtime while the family members urge that employee to come home. In a seminal article, Greenhaus and Beutell (1985) refined the notion of role conflict further and divided work-family conflict into three categories: *time-based*, *strain-based* and *behaviour-based*. Time-based conflicts occur when time spent in one role precludes participation in another role. Strain-based conflicts occur when stressors arising in one role affect the individual's enactment of another role. Behaviour-based conflicts arise from situations where norms or expectations for behaviour in one role are incompatible for behaviour in the other role.

Role conflict is also *bidirectional*. It can be *asymmetric* or *reciprocal*. An example of asymmetric role conflict may be that of a working father who feels that his work role interferes with his family role, yet does not feel that his family role interferes with his work role. An example of reciprocal role conflict involves the case of a working mother who feels that her work life interferes with her family role and her household responsibilities conflict with her work life.

Emerging Models

Past research has contributed to our understanding

of the work-home interface, yet comprehension of psychological and behavioural challenges people face in navigating multiple roles remained inadequate. More recently new perspectives are focusing on the enriching aspects of multiple roles. The new perspective emphasizes the notion of psychological resources. From this perspective it is useful to discuss people's preferences for integrating or segmenting work and family roles.

Enrichment. While role conflict and stress are possible psychological outcomes of participating in multiple roles, another potential psychological consequence of participating in multiple roles is enrichment. The notion is based on the premise that roles provide individuals with psychological resources that can be beneficial to them in other life roles. This research draws its force from sociologist Sieber (1974) and Marks (1977).

Sieber's (1974) concept of *role accumulation* suggests four mechanisms through which individuals benefit from holding multiple roles because they can (a) amass role privileges across their various roles, (b) achieve overall status security by allowing roles to serve as buffers or compensate for each other, (c) receive additional resources for status enhancement and improved role performance, and finally (d) experience personality enrichment and ego gratification through the psychological experience of occupying multiple roles. Marks (1977) posits an expansion model of human energy, allegiance and personal resources through enactment of multiple roles. He argues that enactment of multiple roles creates more energy rather than deplete energy.

Foundational research on the enrichment perspective predicts that participation in multiple roles is significantly related to mental health. Empirical studies indicate that individuals who hold multiple role experience less psychological distress. In another study, undergraduates of a business program participated in the investigation. They provided information regarding their work and non-work roles. The 122 respondents held a variety of non-work roles including community work, recreation groups and families. The study found significant support for the enrichment model. The increased time spent in community work and parenting was associated with greater job satisfaction and organizational commitment.

Rothbard (2001) drew on psychological theories of emotion and self-esteem to explain why positive and negative affect in response to one role might carry over and increase or decrease engagement in another role. She surveyed workers of various types at a large public university in the USA. She found that both enrichment and depletion can occur as a result of engagement in multiple roles. She found gender difference in the effects of engagement. Women's work-related negative affect was depleting to family engagement whereas men's work-related positive affect was enriching to family engagement. Moreover, women's work engagement was positively influenced by both positive and negative family-related affect. Rothbard (2001) suggests that the affective experience of work and family roles are key determinants of whether holding multiple role is enriching or depleting.

A number of studies find that commitment to multiple life roles is positively related to well-being.

Role Boundaries. Past research was addressed to the issues of the permeability of the boundary between home and work. The new perspective focuses explicitly on integration versus segmentation as strategies for coping with work and family roles. *Segmentation is a strategy by which a person separates work and non-work time, artifacts and* *activities whereas integration is a strategy whereby the person overlaps these role experiences.*

Hall (1972) observed female college students who were also mothers and wives. He observed the strategies of integration involves "redesigning roles so that they can be performed simultaneously in a mutually reinforcing manner". Role partitioning is described as "choosing not to attend to one role while performing another".

Consistent with Hall's idea, many investigators find that people actively manage the work non-work boundary using integration or segmentation. Nipper Eng (1995) studied employees at a research and development firm. She found that scientists and other professional workers led very integrated life styles. They handled personal matters such as paying bills or making doctor's appointment during work time. These scientists keep many work-related journals in their homes. There was integration in their management style. Conversely other employees segmented their work and non-work lives. These workers never mentioned their non-work activities at work; they did not take work home any way.

More recent empirical work has shown that segmenting or integrating boundary management strategy is influenced by a few other factors. In one study it was found that the degree of role conflict is a determinant. Rau and Hyland (2002) studied MBA students and found that those with low role conflict were more attracted to companies that offered telecommuting arrangement (a more integrating style), whereas those with high role conflict were more attracted to companies that offered flexi time arrangement (a more segmenting style). This is because integrating might exacerbate the effects of conflict when people have high degrees of role conflict.

Other research has looked into the fit between individuals' preferred style and organizational arrangement. As indicated earlier, individuals have a preferred strategy (integration or segmentation). Yet the preference may not be congruent with organizational policy. When employee preference for how they would like to manage boundary between home and work are incongruent with company policy and practices, employees experience lower satisfaction and commitment.

Identify navigation. Another emerging perspective involves role identity and the ways people navigate multiple role identities. Individual identity is closely related to the roles people hold. Further, the extent to which any individual identifies with a given role affects their enactment of that role as well as role outcomes. Several studies have found support for the effect of role identification on role participation. An investigator surveyed former students of an education course and found that those with a higher career identity reported greater work effort. Similarly it was shown that an increased identification with a family role was associated with greater investment of time in family role.

Role identification appears to be a key factor affecting the outcome of enactment of work and non-work roles. It is plausible that individuals identify unequally with work and non-work roles and that one role will serve as an *anchor identity role*. In other words, the anchor identity role is more salient and central to the individual's self-definition than the other roles they may hold. Further whether or not anchor and non-anchor roles are identity-affirming or identity-discrepant makes a difference. When both the anchor and non-anchor roles are identity-affirming the individual experiences increased enrichment and reduced conflict between roles. When anchor role is identity-affirming and non-anchor role is identity-discrepant, the individual will retreat to the affirming anchor role.

The possibility that individuals might identify differently with their work and non-work roles does not preclude the probability that they can identify equally. One study compared the outcomes of those who identified equally and unequally with their work role and their role in a community-based volunteer orchestra. There was an interaction effect between relative identification and boundary management strategy. Those who identified more equally experienced greater role conflict while integrating rather than segmenting their roles.

Increased corporate globalization brings the issue of role boundary management and identity navigation in the context of demographic diversity. As diverse groups of people come together they must decide how much of their "selves" should be included in their organizations. A study by Phillips et at (2002) has shown that individuals in diverse groups report greater preference for segmentation of work and home roles. Perhaps this is due to the individual's need to preserve their cultural identity.

Measurement Issues

Despite variation in conceptualization, the most common construct is that of work-family conflict. It requires operationalization (measurement). Greenhaus and Beutells's (1985) influential theoretical work articulated different categories of work-family conflict based on directionality and type.

Directionality and Type

The directionality dimension distinguishes between the source of the conflict (work interfering with family and family interfering with work). Most of the early research focused on either broad measure of conflict that includes both directions or just work interfering with family. In a study, it was shown that work interfering with family was reported nearly three times as often as family interfering with work.

Apart from directionality, Greenhaus and Beutell (1985) identified three types of conflict: strain-, time-, and behaviour- based.

Criticism of Conflict Measure

There are other measurement techniques in addition to Greenhaus and Beutell's scale. Yet this one has been used more extensively. Of course, it is not completely problem-free. A general criticism of this technique is its failure to distinguish work-family and work-non-work conflict.

Work-Family Facilitation

As indicated earlier, multiple roles are beneficial to individual well-being. Further recent emphasis on studying 'positive psychology' (Seligman & Csikszentmihalyi, 2000) has stressed the ways in which work and family enhance each other. This work-family facilitation is also bidirectional.

Antecedents of Conflict

In social and behavioural research, it is very difficult to isolate cases and effects. However, certain antecedents can be identified. The model distinguishes between WFI (Work Family Interference) and FWI (Family Work Interference).

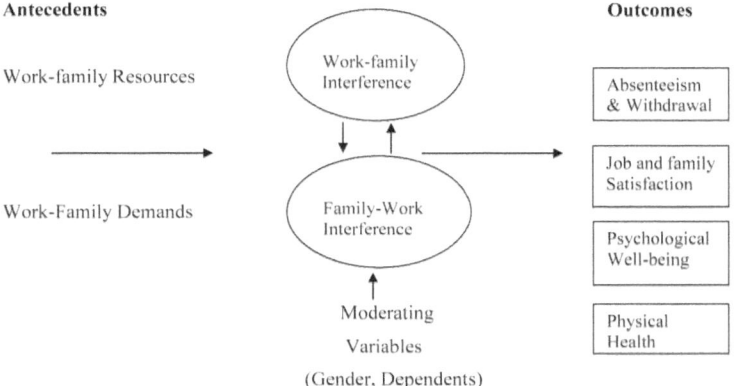

Figure: A Model of Work-Family Interference

Resources

It is postulated that individuals have finite amounts of psychological resources, time and physical energy. Each life role of an individual exerts demands on these finite resources. Stress is experienced when the demands of multiple roles exceed the individual's resources.

A principal characteristic of the role strain hypothesis is the salience or value of each role to an individual. A high value placed upon family life requires the devotion of time and energy to the family domain. If these preferences are blocked by job-related demands, the work-family conflict will occur.

The role of work and family stress as an antecedent of work-family conflict can also be explained by Conservation of Resource Model. The COR model proposes that individuals act to acquire and maintain a variety of resources (objects, energies, conditions, and personal characteristics). Stress occurs when a loss of a resource is threatened or experienced. Work-family conflict occurs when attempts to balance work and home demands lead to the loss of resources from either (or both) domain(s). Individuals who have many resources will experience less stress and conflict, for some resources will act as buffers against stress and conflict. The COR model classifies variables such as gender, marital status, age, job tenure, job rank, and status as resources.

Some of common findings:
- Employed women may have a lower job rank, status and tenure, and thus fewer resources. Consequently, they lead to experience higher levels of work-family conflict than employed men.
- The COR model views having a spouse positively as an additional resource to be drawn upon. Hence married individuals experience lower self-reported family stress than individuals without spouse.
- The number of children an individual has at home is associated with a corresponding loss of the resources of time and energy. This results in stress and FWI. This explains why the number of dependents is a source of conflict.

Work and Family Demands

Carlson and Frone (2003) suggest that work-family conflict is caused by two types of interference between the home and work domains: *internal* and *external interference.* Internal interference is created by self-imposed demands such as standards of excellence that hinder in participation of home life, and vice versa. External interference occurs when a source external to the individual is operative. For example, a work deadline may prevent an individual's participation in home life. Similarly, family responsibilities may reduce attendance in work. Thus, internal and external sources may contribute to four types of interference.

Exhibit: Four Types of Interference

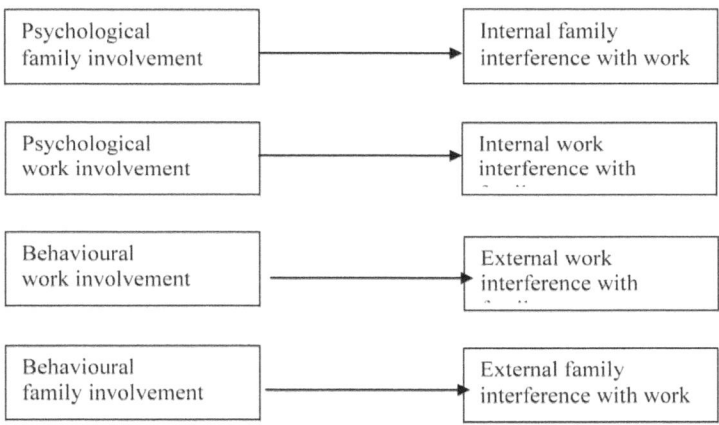

A major predictor of behavioural involvement in both the family and work domain is time demands. As time demands in a domain increase the level of behavioural involvement in that domain also increases. This results in less behavioural involvement in the other domain, thus producing conflict. In a study, it was found that work hours were associated with external WFI. As the time spent at work increased so did the experience of WFI. Another study found that increased family involvement was associated with internal FWI. The amount of thought about family life while at work interfered with work performance.

An interesting corollary of the time pressure is the application of time management. Three time management techniques (setting goals and priorities, energy in time management and general organization activities) predict levels of work-family conflict. For instance, engaging in time management may induce a perception that one is in control over work and family demands. This, in turn, reduces feelings of conflict between these domains.

Consequences of Work-Family Conflict

A group of researchers have suggested that there are three groups of consequences: work-related outcomes, non-work-related outcomes, and stress-related outcomes.

Work-related Outcomes

In general, these outcomes include job satisfaction, commitment, turnover intention, absenteism, performance and success. Work-family conflict is positively related to work absenteism and turnover intention. While both forms of conflict positively predict turnover intention, WFI produced a stronger relationship. Both directions of conflict produce withdrawal behaviour from both the work and family domains.

A consequence of work-family conflict also involves reduction in job satisfaction.

Non-work-related Outcomes

Non-work-related outcomes include marital, family, leisure and life satisfaction and family performance. WFI is linked with reduced family / marital satisfaction and FWI results in decreased job satisfaction. Life satisfaction is a combination of both family and job satisfaction, and therefore spans both work and family domains. Life satisfaction and work-family conflict have a strong negative relationship.

Stress-related Outcomes

Stress-related outcomes include psychological strain, physical health, depression, substance use and burn out. Associations between work-family conflict and psychological distress have been widely supported. Relationships between work-family conflict and depression have also been demonstrated. Typically, experiences of both types of work-family conflict produce increased depression and this association is similar for both men and women. Recent research suggests a negative association between levels of conflict and physical health. It is shown that dual demands of both paid employment and care giving are associated with physical strain symptoms such as weight loss, head ache, drowsiness and insomnia. The strain imposed by work-family conflict has also been linked to coronary heart disease, decreased appetite, increased fatigue, nervous tension and anxiety.

Work-Family Facilitation

Much of the past research was directed to discuss how work and family demands can be sources of conflict and stress. In recent years, aspects of facilitation have been recognized. It is suggested that work and family can also be a source of strength to one another. For instance, support from members of one's own family can be source of strength when faced with demanding job challenges.

Different terms have been used to refer to the facilitative process through which one domain positively influences the other. The term work-family enhancement has been used by some authors. Other authors have referred to *positive spillover* between work and family. There is also reference to work-family compensation and work-family enrichment. A close scrutiny of these terms reveals considerable content overlap, although subtle differences remain.

It is important to identify some antecedents of facilitation. Grzywacz (2002) suggests four types of antecedents. These include: (a) individual dispositional characteristics, (b) exploitable family work-related resources, (c) selective permeability of family and workplace boundaries, and (d) demand characteristics.

Individual Dispositional Characteristics

Grzywacz (2002) has argued that work-family facilitation can be initiated and sustained by developmentally generative disposition characteristics. These include innovativeness, openness and conscientiousness. Some investigators found that conscientiousness and agreeableness are positively related to work-family facilitation but not to work-family conflict. It suggests that facilitation and conflict have different origins.

Exploitable Resources

According to Clark (2000), two contextual factors central to the work-family linkage are the availability of resources (materials, assets or commodities in the environment, interpersonal support). The salary paid to the employee is an economic resource. Social support is a by-product of family. The extent to which resources are exploitable increases the possibility of facilitation. An example involves the ability of skilled professionals to transfer knowledge and skills to their children through informal family interactions.

Selective Boundary Permeability

Grzywacz (2002) has posited that selective boundary

permeability is required for work-family facilitation to occur. Work-family facilitation is more likely to occur when resources in one domain (e.g. work) are exploitable and can be utilized in the other domain (e.g. family). An example would be decision making. Investigators find a strong correlation between high levels of decision latitudes in the job and work-to-family facilitation.

Demand Characteristics

Certain attributes of individuals elicit specific responses from the social environment that either promote or undermine work-family facilitation. Gender provides a good illustration of the impact of socially constructed demand characteristics. Owing to gender role expectation concerning family responsibilities, women are more likely than men to scale back their career and working hours to accommodate family demands and to balance work and family. Hence, demand characteristics such as gender role expectations may elicit differential opportunity for individuals to maintain work-family balance.

In a study, Sahoo and Bidyadhar (1994) investigated whether separate set of critical factors emerge as significant for work-family harmony and work-family conflict. The findings of their study showed that emotional support from spouse, child maintenance facilities and clarity of division of duty emerged as significant harmony-inducing factors for both males and females. Similarly, temperamental differences emerged as highly significant conflict-enhancing parameter for both males and females. However, family demands and work obligations were given significant weightages by females only. These findings appear relevant especially in Indian socio-cultural setting.

Summary and Implications

The contemporary research on work-life integration has generated several conceptual models and useful perspectives. A number of measurement techniques have also been developed. The two key issues involves work-family conflict and work-family facilitation. The empirical findings on these interface suggest a number of important implications for achieving balance.

The first step is to examine the stressors that cause work-family conflict. Some of the stressors have been identified and it requires collaboration between employees and management in handling these stressors. Similarly, antecedents (resources) of facilitation have been identified. Yet, determination of the magnitude of these stressors and resources is required prior to undertaking intervention programs for attainment of balance. In addition to the identification of specific stressors and resources as antecedent variables, the delineation of moderators (buffers) is also required. These pragmatic steps and supportive intervention programmes would be helpful in achieving work-life integration.

Chapter 9

Workplace Spirituality

Spirituality was a topic that was considered inappropriate for social and behavioural research. Many behavioural scientists viewed spirituality as a core concern of philosophers. However, world scenarios and business climate in recent times have stressed the urgent need of discussion and practice of spirituality in workplace.

Some people, of course, feel skeptical about whether spirituality can mix with work. Others feel apprehensive that some religious pressure will be put on them at work. Still others feel enthused at the possibility of spirituality revolution at work. The word "revolution" has two meanings. The first is the fundamental revolution. The other definition is equally important. What does the earth do every 24 hours? It completes one revolution, returning to where it began. The second meaning of revolution is to "return to where you began".

Humanity went through both types of revolution when the astronauts first went to the moon. Revolutionary technologies were manifest. An equally fundamental shift took place in our consciousness. Edgar Mitchell, an American astronaut on the Apollo 14 flight, said:

"The powerful experience of seeing the Earth and our whole solar system against the background of the cosmos had a very profound effect on me, an overwhelming sense of being connected with the universe, of feeling connected to all things.... We went to the moon as technicians, we returned as humanitarians".

Defining Spirituality

Although most people describe themselves as spiritual, they define the term in many different ways. Experts also vary in their definitions. An internet search reveals more than 500 definitions of spirituality. Some of the oft-quoted definitions are given below:

- The best of that which is human
- A quest for existential meaning
- The transcendental human dimensions

However, Pergament and Mahoney (2005) define spirituality as a *search for the sacred*. There are two key terms in this definition: search and the sacred. The term search indicates that spirituality is a process; it involves efforts to discover the sacred. People can take a virtually limitless number of pathways in their attempts to discover and preserve the sacred. Spiritual pathways may range from traditional religious institutions to nontraditional avenues.

While religion and spirituality were used interchangeably in the long past, the clarity of distinction between the two has been attained in recent times. Religion represents an institutional, formal, outward, doctrinal and authoritarian system. In contrast, spirituality denotes an individual, subjective, emotional and inward expression.

In recent years psychologists have carried out a large numbers of studies to examine the relationship religious experience and mental health. Findings are perplexing. Some studies indicate a positive association between them, while other show negative relationship. So psychologists have distinguished two forms of religious experiences: *external religiosity* and *internal religiosity*. External religiosity is indicated in the form of attending the place of worships, rituals and other outward behaviours. Internal religiosity refers to attitude and values. Accordingly, spirituality has been likened to internal religiosity.

Spirituality, defined as a search for sacredness, not only highlights the search process; it also involves efforts to hold onto the sacred once it has been discovered. People can take a number of routes to discover and conserve the sacred.

What are the roots of this discovery process? Some point to the role of innate genetic basis. Others have pointed out the role of critical life events. The challenges people face face may reveal human limitation and prompt them to seek out the sacred. In addition, the social context including the family, institution and crucial milieu play important roles in stimulating the discovery process.

The search process or sanctification holds three important implications for our lives. First we are likely to preserve and protect sacred objects. Second, we are likely to invest more of ourselves in pursuit of the sacred. Third, we are likely to derive more meaning, strength and satisfaction from sacred of our lives.

Spiritual Intelligence

The systematic approach towards the study of spirituality has centered around the construct of *spiritual intelligence*. The evolution of interest in this area has also followed a logical sequence of events. It is a known fact that both researchers and change agents were interested in the study of *rational intelligence* during early part of the twentieth century. They measured intelligence operationally and expressed intellectual capacity in form of intelligent quotient (IQs). IQs were regarded as stable and strong predictors of academic attainments and professional success.

However, mid 90's brought a drastic change in these scenarios. Goleman's (1991) book *emotional Intelligence* popularized the concept of emotional *quotient (EQ)*. This was strengthened by the neuro–psychological finding that our brain, though structurally one, has two functional units – *feeling brain and thinking brain*. In evolutionary terms, feeling brain is older than the thinking brain. The noble – prize winning physiologist Roger Sperry (1981) showed that left hemisphere of the brain is linked with logic and language while right hemisphere is associated with emotion and pattern recognition. EQ is a basic requirement for the effective use of IQ. If "feeling" areas of the brain is damaged, we *think* less effectively.

Thus, the primacy of emotional intelligence was recognized in 1970's. Compared with rational intelligence, EQ was considered as a stronger predictor of academic and occupational success. But the turn of the century signaled another interesting and enduring development. The construct that unifies rational intelligence and emotional intelligence was advanced to explain our search for meaning and values.

Spiritual intelligence refers to that intelligence with which we place our actions and lives wider, richer and meaning–giving context. **It is a necessary foundation for the effective functioning of both IQ and EQ.**

Webster dictionary defines *spirit* as "the vital principle, which gives life to physical organism in contrast to its material elements." In other words, it is "the breath of life".

The spiritual intelligence prompts us to ask fundamental questions. !Why am I born? What is the purpose of my life? What are my worthwhile goals? Anthropologists and neurologists argue that it is this longing for meaning and its evolutionary value that have prompted humans to come out of caves. This longing is also responsible for the growth of human brain.

Neither IQ nor EQ, separately or in combination, is enough to explain the full complexity of human intelligence. IQ and EQ play finite games, whereas SQ plays infinite games. SQ has no necessary connection to religion. For some people, SQ may find a mode of expression through formal religion, but being religious does not guarantee SQ.

Scientific Evidence

A great deal of scientific evidence for SQ does exist. In recent years, neurological, psychological and anthropological studies of human intelligence and linguistic process offer supportive evidence.

First, in the early 1990's, a neuropsychologist Michael Persinger found that temporal lobe activity was linked with mystical visions. More recently, a neurologist V.S. Ramachandran at the University of California identified a built–in spiritual center located among neural connections in the temporal lobes of the brain. Ramachandran (1997) labeled this center 'God spot'. On scans taken with positron emission tomography (PET) these neural areas light up whenever research subjects are exposed to discussions of spiritual or religious topics. These vary with cultures. Westerners respond to mention of 'God'. Easterners respond to symbols meaningful to them. It may be indicated that PET scan is one of the modern imaging techniques. Though injection a harmless radioactive substance is passed to the neural areas of the brain. The concentration of this a substance is deep in those areas of brain which is involved in a particular activity at a given point of time. Of course, the God spot does not prove the existence of God, but it shows that brain has evolved to ask "ultimate questions" to have and to use a sensitivity to wider meaning and values.

Second, the work of Austrian neurologist Wolf Singer in the 1990's on the binding problem shows that there is neural process in the brain devoted to unifying and giving meaning to our experience. It is the neural process that literally 'binds' our experiences together. Prior to singer's work on unifying, synchronous neural oscillations across the whole brain, neurologists and cognitive scientists only recognized two forms of brain neural organization. One of these forms, serial neural connections, is the basis of our IQ. Serially connected neural tracts allow the brain to follow rules, to think logically and rationally step – by – step. In the second form, bundles of up to a hundred thousand neurons are connected in haphazard fashion to other massive bundles. These neural networks are the basis of EQ.

Both serial and parallel computers exist and have different functions, but neither kind operate with meaning. No existing computer can ask 'why'? Singer's work on unifying neural oscillations offers the first hint of a third king of thinking, unitive thinking and an accompanying third mode of intelligence, SQ. Spiritual intelligence can deal with fundamental questions of why, questions of meaning.

Third, Harvard neurologist and biological anthropologist Terrace Deacon has recently published articles dealing with origin of human language (*the Symbolic Species*, 1997). Deacon shows that language is a uniquely human, essentially symbolic, meaning giving activity that coevolved with rapid development in the brain's frontal lobes. Neither existing computers nor even higher apes (with rare and limited exception) can use language, because they lack the frontal lobe facility for dealing with meaning.

Operational Parameters of SQ

In evolutionary terms, SQ has 'wired' us to become the people we are and gives us the potential for further 'rewiring' for growth and transformation. We use SQ to deal with existential problems. SQ is our compass 'at the edge'. Life's most challenging existential problems exist outside the expected and the familiar, outside the given rules, beyond past experience, beyond known skills. In chaos theory, 'the edge' is the border between order and chaos, between the known and the unknown. It is the place where we can be at our most creative. SQ, our deep intuitive sense of meaning and values, is our guide at the edge. SQ is at our conscience. We use SQ to be creative. We call upon it when we need to be flexible, visionary or creatively spontaneous.

We can use SQ to become more spiritually intelligent about religion. SQ takes us to the heart of things, to the unity behind differences. A person high in SQ might practice any religion, but without narrowness and prejudice. Similarly, a person high in SQ could have many spiritual qualities without being religious at all.

SQ allows us to integrate the intrapersonal and interpersonal. It helps to transcend the gap between self – and others. Although emotional intelligence includes both components (interpersonal skill and intrapersonal skill), SQ is needed to bridge the gap between the two.

Finally, we can use our SQ to solve the problems of good and evil, problems of life and death, the deepest origins of human suffering. The indicators of highly developed SQ incl;ude the following:

- ❖ The capacity to be flexible
- ❖ A high degree of self – awareness
- ❖ A capacity to face and use suffering
- ❖ A capacity to face and transcend pain
- ❖ The quality of being inspired by vision and values
- ❖ A reluctance to cause unnecessary harm
- ❖ A tendency to see unity in diversity
- ❖ A tendency to ask 'why'? or what if? Questions and to seek fundamental answers

Pragmatic Strategies

Correlated with growth of interest in spiritual intelligence, workplace spirituality began as a movement in the early 1990s. it emerged as a grassroots movement with individuals seeking to live their faith and/ or spiritual values in the workplace. Soon after many organizations sprang up to further such movement.

- ➢ International Centre for *Spirit* at Warm(www.spiritatwork.org)
- ➢ World Business academy (www.worldbusiness.org)
- ➢ Spiritual Business Network (www.spiritualbusiness.net)
- ➢ Foundation for Workplace Spirituality (www.workplacespirituality.org.uk)

In the late 1990s, the Academy of Management (www.aomonline.org) formed a special interest group called the Management, Spirituality and Religion Interest Group. This is a professional association of management professors from all over the world who are teaching and doing research on spirituality and religion in the workplace. This action by the Academy of Management was a significant step in legitimizing workplace spirituality in the workplace as a field of study

Similarly, the Division 36 of the American Psychological Association (Psychology of Religion and Spirituality) has launched a new Journal in 2008 to reflect the wave of interest. Research carried out in India is disseminated through global Dharma Center (www.globaldharma.org) and Times of India (www.http//spirituality.indiatimes.com).

The International Center for spirituality and work provides an operational definition.

Spirituality is an innate human attribute. All people bring this as an integral part of themselves to the workplace. Spirituality is a state or experience that can provide individuals with direction or meaning or provide feelings of understanding, support, inner wholeness or correctedness. Correctedness can be to themselves, other people, nature, the universe, a God, or some other supernatural power.

The definition implies both a vertical component and a horizontal component. The *vertical component* represents a desire to transcend the individual ego or personal self. The vertical component might be God, Spirit, Universe, Nature, Higher Power or something else. This dimension is experienced as a conscious sense of profound connection to the Universe/ God/ Spirit. This might be experienced internally as moments of awe or peak experiences. A strong sustained vertical component reflects outer behaviours as person (group) who is centered and able to tap into deep inner strength and wisdom. Generally quiet time in nature or other reflective activities or practices are required. Examples include meditation rooms, time for shared reflection, silence before meetings, prayer and support for employees to take time off for spiritual development.

The horizontal component represents a desire to be of service to other humans and the planet. In the horizontal we seek to make difference through our actions. A strong horizontal component is demonstrated by a service orientation, compassion and well- aligned visions and values. A person with both strong vertical and horizontal components has a clear grasp of mission, ethics and activities.

Spirituality in the workplace means that employees find nourishment for both the vertical and horizontal dimensions. It is about individuals and organizations seeing work as a spiritual path as an opportunity to grow and to contribute to society in a meaningful way. It is about care, compassion and support of others, about integrity and people being true to themselves. It means individuals and organizations attempting to live their values more fully in the work they do. Examples of vertical organizational spirituality include meditation time at the beginnings of meetings, retreat or spiritual training time set aside for employees, and appropriated accommodation of employee prayer practices. Companies with strong sense of horizontal spirituality take care of the following: caring behaviour among coworkers, a societal responsibility orientation, strong service commitment to customers, environmental sensitivity and community service activity. The vertical and horizontal; dimensions should be well –integrated so that motivation (stemming from the vertical) and actions (springing from the horizontal) are explicitly linked.

The drive to create a more spiritual work environment has taken steps. By and large the following activities are included.

- Bereavement programs
- Wellness information displayed and distributed
- Employee Assistance Programs
- Programs that integrate work/ family
- Management systems that encourage personal and spiritual transformation
- Servant leadership – the desire to serve others
- Stewardship – leadership that supports growth and well – being of others
- Diversity programs that create inclusive cultures
- Integration of core values and core business decision and practices

The drive to make difference in the world takes forms of practice mainly at three levels: Individual, leader and organization. The discussion of specific strategies at these three levels brings clarity to an understanding of practice components of workplace spirituality.

Individual Efforts

Spirituality at workplace takes a tangible form only when individuals, leaders and organizations work harmoniously towards such goals. Individuals need to develop *spiritual character* in the workplace. Spiritual character is denoted by the following equation.

$$\text{Spiritual Character} = \frac{\text{Spiritual context} + \text{Spiritual purpose} + \text{Spiritual values}}{\text{Ego desires}}$$

As indicated by the expression, individuals need to work in the context spiritualized by supportive belief system. Individuals ought to believe that collective good is possible through spiritual means. This is further by spiritual goal or purpose. Moreover, spiritual values are to be sought. Of course, spiritual values are basically human values such as truth (*satya*), righteousness (*dharma*), peace (*shanti*), love (*prema*) and nonviolence (*ahimsa*). Here again love is the unifying force. Words soaked with love constitute truth. Action with love gives rise to righteousness. Emotion saturated with love generates peace. Understanding with love takes the form of nonviolence. When individuals integrate their words, thoughts, emotion and action with the love, human values are preserved and promoted. The other guiding principle for the individual is the responsiveness to conscience – an inner prompting. People may encounter some situations where organizational decision conflicts with individuals' moral consideration. In such difficult situations, people with spiritual character listen to the dictates of their conscience. At the call of conscience, many individuals have ventured to oppose the immoral and corrupt practices of the organization.

The rich tradition of Indian heritage advises people 'to start early, drive slowly and reach safely'. Spiritual teachers of India have advised to make an early beginning. A small increment every day may be very helpful.

While practicing spirituality at workplace one has to view spirituality on the basis of success. Workplace spirituality is not a one – way street. It is a two – way street. One has to work to grow spiritually and growing spiritually is instrumental for working better. Finally, one has to talk one's thought and walk one's talk. Individual attempts are strongly facilitated by spiritually based leaders.

Spiritual Leader

Anyone who expresses his or her spiritual Self with

confidence can be spiritual leader, whether they influence one or ten or a hundred other. Spirituality based leaders exhibit four key faculties.

- They have a clearly held spiritual view of life. They have a clear definition of spirituality; they know their own relationship between spirituality and religion. They continually ask. "How can I approach this situation from my spiritual view of life?"
- They explore their spirituality from inside. Carl Jung remarked "He who looks outside dreams, he who looks inside awakes". Such a leader looks into his or her heart. They take consistent time to nurture their spiritual growth, they identify their spiritual purpose and values in life and continuously check up on their purity and unity of thought, action and words.
- They embody their spiritual principles in their leadership. They see spirituality as the basis of their success. They appreciate work in terms of spiritual opportunity and spiritual growth. They seek to "talk their thought" and "walk their thought".
- They engage in revolutionary activity. They promote fundamental change based on their spiritual view of life.

When an executive operates his or her business from a spiritual point of view, does it change their definition of the "bottom line?" The term "bottom line" originally meant the last line of an income statement, the profits that remained after costs were deducted from revenues. Over time, it has come to mean something broad, "the key result" or the "most important outcomes" of an enterprise.

When we focus on spiritual – based measures of a "bottom line", we are more likely to stay uplifted in our vision. We are more likely to see beyond the profit motive, beyond even the self – interest of the organization and beyond even the welfare of the society in material terms. We are likely to become embodiment of Spirit who can see what is eternally important and make sure the time and energy we spend at work truly contributes to what's ultimately important.

In addition to effort of spiritually based leaders, organizations need to adopt some useful practices in this direction.

Organizational Soul

Since the fall of Enron and Worldcom, corporate scandals have taken their toll on the conscience of the business world. Today, people want to do business with companies that have strong moral values. The challenge for business, however, is creating a caring value – based atmosphere without it negatively affecting their bottom line. Dr. Margaret Benefiel's new book, *Soul at work,* says that not only can collective spirituality make for happier employees – it can also boost business profits.

Benefiel argues that spirituality and profitability can be combined so that these two goals work in synergy. She writes, "spiritually grounded organizations perform better and better enrich their stakeholders". She urges others to follow a new business model and reap enormous rewards that are more than financial. Synergy can be attained by adopting certain routes.

Articulate Values. It is possible to attend to soul by including precise language in their vision and mission statements. For example, Document Management Group's (Dublin. Ireland) vision statement includes a commitment to build a workplace in which "our people can find meaning, significance and success through their work, and where personal and workplace values align to achieve greater outward harmony and spiritual life". The harmony between financial concerns and human concerns leads to healthier happier organizations.

Match People with Mission. The caring environment must find people with similar wavelengths. Southwest Airlines (USA), for example, hires for attitude and trains for skills. It is believed that the congruence with their mission would heighten employee retention and customer satisfaction. This would lower costs and boost profits.

Special Activity of Personnel Division. The importance attached to organizational soul can take manifest forms. The personnel wing of the organization needs to devote time and energy in training employees to integrate – spirituality with their work behaviour.

Create Specific structure and Processes. Structure and practices can be adopted to further spirituality at workplace. For example, at Grayston Foundation in New York, a moment of silence punctuates business meetings, and the senior management team takes quarterly daylong retreat off sites. Texas Instruments has provided Serenity Rooms" where employees experience calm moments. This strengthens the harmony between financial goals and human concerns.

Conclusion

The discussion on workplace spirituality does not rule out the possibility of critic's comments. However, most of the critics point out the elements of conflict and confusion arising our religious practices in organization. The critics argue that spirituality and religious practices are matter of personal beliefs and these must not be allowed to play their role in organizations. They apprehend that a such climate would dilute and distort organizational goal. Yet, a close and thoughtful examination of present crisis and uncertainties deepen our impression that a hunger for spiritual climate is likely to solve the problem of self-interest. The preservation and promotion of common goods is sure to be facilitated by a spiritual revolution taking its roots in present day workplaces.

Chapter 10

Androgyny and Work Behaviour

The quality of life is fundamental concern of every society. All societies strive for their citizen's enrichment of activity experiences. However, this objective presents a formidable challenge. Because of complexity of societal structure and global events, many factors complicate the process of social planning. Every society is like an organism. Its origin, growth, and enrichment are influenced by elements that constitute it. Men and women are elementary units of a society. The characteristics of men and women greatly influence the nature and quality of society.

Both men and women, in turn, are products of ongoing changes of external reality. The various roles they perform, the activities they endorse, and the ideals they emulate shape their behavioural patterns. In recent years, there are many events that have transformed the conventional standards regarding men and women. More specifically, women liberation movement and greater participation of women in workforce have brought about some tangible changes in developed societies. Similarly, a transition from rural and agricultural lifestyle to urban industrialized pattern has modified standards regarding sex-appropriate roles in developing countries.

During the last few decades, the traditional society of India has been undergoing a series of changes. Multi-directional forces of urbanization, industrialization and socio-educational advancement are affecting various aspects of traditional Indian society. More recently, changes have become more pronounced as a result of political independence, constitutional measures, planned economic development, programmes of industrialization and social development, emergence of urban culture, western science and technology, secularization and rational outlook. The changes in socio-economic political conditions have brought out changes in beliefs, attitudes, and value system.

In this transitional state of changing environment, both men and women are experiencing a psychological change in themselves. It is our fundamental concern to examine the pattern of these changing values, attitudes and roles, particularly in the context of present situation.

Traditional View of Gender Stereotypes

Stereotypes is the belief system containing generalization about the characteristics of the group of persons. The term gender-stereotype is usually considered to be cognitive. It is a set of beliefs, it deals with what men and women are alike and it is shared by the members of a particular group. Gender stereotypes consist of those psychological characteristics of behavioural traits that are believed to characterize men with greater frequency or lesser frequency than they characterize women. According to William and Best (1982), gender roles (e.g., that there are more men than women engineers) are often explained by reference to gender stereotypes (e.g., men are strong).

The behaviours which are labeled as masculine and feminine are not inevitable consequences of biological differences between males and females. Masculine and feminine behaviours are culturally prescribed. Youngsters are socialized in the work activities and personality characteristics defined as differentially appropriate for males are females in their own culture. Every one of us is so familiar with the social roles that there is no need to point specifically that behaviour patterns expected of males are considerably same in almost all the cultures of the world. Similarly, behaviour patterns expected of females are also considerably same across many cultures.

Exhibit 1: Some Gender Stereotypes

Males	Female
Masculine	Feminine
Ambitious	Affectionate
Competitive	Cooperative
Athletic	Cheerful
Assertive	Childlike
Dominant	Sympathetic

Gender stereotypes not only affect the occupational opportunities of adult men and women, but at a much earlier age, may also determine the manner in which adults respond to younger generations, thus influencing the budding adults' perception of their behaviour, talents and traits and their expectations for their future adult life.

The different studies in gender stereotypes stimulated the curiosity to study many interesting facts concerning the nature of traits of males and females. Soon after the studies of gender stereotypes, people became interested to know the definition of an *adequate person*. Gradually it surfaced that an adequate person or an 'androgynous' person is one who is both masculine and feminine, both assertive and yielding and both instrumental and expressive, depending upon the situational appropriateness of these various behaviours.

The Emerging Concept of Androgyny

The concept of androgyny individual (form andro-male, gyne-female) denotes a person who does not rely on gender as a cognitive organizing principle. Such an individual combines both masculine and feminine elements.

Androgyny allows the individual to be both independent and tender, assertive and yielding, masculine and feminine. It greatly expands the range of behaviour open to everyone, permitting people to cope more effectively with diverse situations. The concept of androgyny proposes that instead of conceiving of masculinity and femininity as a duality, one should consider that any individual may have both masculine and feminine personality components regardless of gender.

Sandra Bem is credited with the scientific articulation of the construct. In the course of her class room interaction, she asked her graduate students to prepare a list of traits commonly found in males. Student generated a list of masculine stereotypes. When asked to generate a list of traits commonly found in females, students prepared a list of feminine stereotypes. Then Bem asked students to prepare another list (List 3) containing traits generally found in men but desirable for both men and women. Interestingly students prepared such a list containing traits such as ambitious, competitive, assertive. Similarly, when asked, students generated list 4 containing traits generally found in women but describle for both men and women. Such a list contained traits such as sympathetic, affectionate, cooperative and childlike. The whole exercise deepened the impression that an adequate person blends within himself or herself the positive qualities of both men and women. On the basis of such conceptualization, Bem devised a psychometric measure of androgyny.

Measurement

Sandra Bem devised a sex role inventory (Bem's Sex Role Inventory or BSRI). She treated masculinity and femininity as two independent dimensions and thereby make it possible to characterize a person an masculine, feminine, androgynous or undifferentiated as a function of the difference between his or her endorsement of masculine and feminine characteristics. Items were selected by student judges and were assigned to the masculinity and femininity scales if there judged to be more desirable for one sex or the other. The male and female stereotypes defined in Bem's method are generally similar to those found in other societies reflecting the usual male instrumentality and female expressiveness. The BSRI is a paper-

Exhibit 2: Classification of Types

	Masculinity	
	Low	High
Femininity High	Feminine	Androgynous
Femininity Low	Undifferentiated	Masculine

Pencil instrument. It includes both a masculinity scale and a femininity scale, each of which containing 20 personality characteristics selected on the basis of gender-typed social desirability.

When taking BSRI, a person is asked to indicate on a 7-point scale how well each of these masculine and feminine personality characteristics describes himself/herself. The scale ranges from 1 (never or almost never true) and to 7 (always or almost always true) and is labeled at each point. On the basis of his or her responses, each person receives androgyny score defined as the difference between his or her endorsement of masculine and feminine characteristics. Smaller is the differences greater is the magnitude of androgyny (of course, excepting the cases when both masculinity score and femininity score are very low).

Although BSRI is an oft-used measure of androgyny, its cultural appropriateness may be challenged. The masculinity and femininity scores (based on BSRI) obtained from Indian participants are not likely to be accurate expressions. With a view to offering a meaningful operationalization, a culturally valid measure was needed.

Sahoo (2004) developed a culturally valid measure of androgyny. For the development and validation of this scale Sahoo's Sex Role Inventory (SSRI) followed similar format of BSRI. It consisted of 20 masculine items and 20 feminine items. Participants are asked to indicate an a 7-point scale the extent to which each descriptor is characteristic of himself or herself. At the time of scoring, masculinity, femininity and neutral items are considered separately. The sum of endorsement ratings of an individual across all masculine items indicates his or her masculinity score. Similarly, the sum of ratings across all neutral items indicates social desirability scores (see Appendix).

Gap between masculinity and femininity sore is indicative of sex role orientation of an individual. The lower is the gap, higher is the level of androgyny (excepting the case where both masculinity and femininity scores are very low). A high difference score in the direction of masculinity indicates masculine stereotype. A high difference score in the direction of femininity score indicates feminine stereotypes. The reliability and validity of the scale is reported elsewhere (Sahoo, 2004).

Androgyny and Behavioural Flexibility

An androgynous person is able to engage in masculine-feminine or a blend of these characteristics depending upon what is appropriate for the specific situation. This flexibility leads to more adaptive behaviour. Bem assessed that only an androgynous person should be able to exhibit flexibility across situations. In a study, Bem and Lenny hypothesized that androgynous persons' flexibility would help them to feel comfortable about performing either masculine or feminine activities. Traditional gender-typed persons tended to show more avoidance of either gender-typed tasks that androgynous persons. Gender-typing was shown to be associated with less effectiveness in cross-sex tasks.

LaFrance and Carmen (1980) observed frequencies of gender-typed nonverbal behaviour during discussions with an instrumental or expressive behaviour. The analysis indicates that responses of androgynous persons revealed cohesiveness of behaviours within type (masculine or feminine), less cross-sex avoidance, less difference between display of each type of behaviours across situations, and fewer extremes of behaviours.

Androgyny represents an ideal of human functioning, blending the best of masculinity and femininity. It is suggested that a combination of masculinity and femininity provide maximum benefits rather than adherence of gender-typical standards. It is reported that androgynous persons consistently rate themselves higher on psychological health and self-concept scales than did those in other gender-role categories.

Androgyny and Work Involvement

The behavioural flexibility demonstrated by androgynous individuals posits a predication that androgyny is positively related to work involvement. Sahoo and Rout (1990) examined such hypothesized relationship and found supportive evidence. The results clearly evinced that androgynous individuals experience greater satisfaction of their salient needs compared to gender-typed individuals. This is consistent with the observation that androgynous individuals are less constrained by gender role stereotypes in their performance and execution of task activities.

A greater degree adaptation to the demands of work setting helps androgynous individuals to experience satisfaction. The androgynous individuals also demonstrate greater degree of work involvement (motivation) compared to gender-typed individuals. As indicated earlier, androgynous individuals have wider range of behavioural orientation, possibility of greater cross-sex behaviour makes it likely that they have higher work involvement. On the contrary, gender-typed individuals show rigid compartmentalization an their behaviour and are likely to restrict their cognitive value of work into a limited range. Persons are said to be wok involved when they perceive performance central to their self-esteem and consistent with their self-concept. The literature on work motivation shows that work involved persons have higher self-esteem and positive self-concept. It is plausible that androgynous individuals are more work involved as they enjoy high self-esteem and positive self-concept owing to a fine blend of masculine and feminine attribute.

Further, the finding that androgynous individuals are better work-involved can be supported by Bem and Lenney's study. That found that androgynous individuals display masculine independence when under pressure to conform. Since androgynous persons more readily than gender-typed individuals respond to situational requirements androgynous persons are more likely to demonstrate adaptiveness to work norms. With a combination of instrumental and expressive orientation and high self-esteem behavioural flexibility, and cross-sex behaviour, androgynous individuals experience greater motivation towards work situation and finally become more involved in their work life.

It is suggested that socialization process be geared to the goal of integrating masculine and feminine characteristics in an individual so that work efficiency and resulting work involvement would be attained.

APPENDIX
Sahoo Sex-Role Inventory (SSRI)

Name .... Age ....
Sex .... Address ....
....
....
....
Occupation ....
                          Date ....

On the opposite side of this sheet, you would find listed a number of characteristics. We would like you to use these *Characteristics to describe yourself*. More specifically, we would like you to indicate, on a scale from 1 to 7, how true of you each of these characteristics is. Please do not leave any characteristic unmarked. Your response would be kept confidential, and would be used only for research.

Thank you for your cooperation.

Example: Clever

Write 1, if it is never or almost never true that you are clever.
Write 2, if it is not usually true that you are clever.
Write 3, if it is sometimes but infrequently true that you are clever.
Write 4, if it is occasionally true that you are clever.
Write 5, if it is often true that you are clever.
Write 6, if it is usually true that you are clever.
Write 7, if it is always or almost true that you are clever.

Thus, if you feel it is often true that you are clever, always or almost always true that you are competent, it is never true that you are silly, and occasionally true that you are hardworking, then you would rate these characteristics are follows:

Clever	5
Computer	7

Silly	1
Hardworking	4

Never or almost never true	Usually not true	Sometimes but infrequently true	Occasionally true	Often true	Usually true	Always or almost always true

Clear-thinking
Innocent
Playful
Attractive
Calculating
Masculine
Productive
Tender
Inventive
Progressive
Takes Initiative
Mild
Optimistic
Likes Security
Realistic
Fashionable
Kind
Imaginative
Frank
Expressive
Affectionate
Energetic
Fair-minded
Charming
Courageous

Active
Daring
Insightful
Has Leadership Ability
Methodical
Loves Children
Modest
Loving
Industrious
Concerned About Group Harmony
Strong Personality
Competitive
Eager To Sooth Hurt Feelings
Dependent
Ambitious
Emotional
Individualistic
Aggressive
Willing To Take A Stand
Courteous
Feminine
Independent
Intellectual
Flatterable
Soft Hearted

Dynamics of Personal Growth | 115

Scoring and Interpretation

Below are listed 20 masculine item and 20 feminine items. Sum your self-endorsement scores across 20 masculine items. That would denote your Masculinity score (M-Score). Similarly sum your ratings across 20 feminine scores. That is indicative of your Feminine Score (F-Score). Find the difference between your M-Score and F-Score. The difference is indicative of your androgyny score. Smaller is the difference between the two, greater is the degree of androgyny.

Masculine Item	Feminine Item
Masculine	Feminine
Ambitious	Love Children
Independent	Likes Security
Courageous	Dependent
Daring	Charming
Methodical	Mild
Energetic	Eager to soothe hurt feelings
Industrious	Flatterable
Takes Initiative	Kind
Progressive	Loving
Intellectual	Clear thinking
Aggressive	Modest
Active	Fashionable
Has Leadership ability	Soft-hearted
Productive	Tender
Inventive	Innocent
Strong Personality	Emotional
Realistic	Affectionate
Willing to take a stand	Attractive
Competitive	Concerned about group harmony

Note: The test SSRI occurs in the book: Sahoo, F.M. (2004). *Sex role in transition*. New Delhi: Kalpaz.

Chapter 11

Workplace Well-Being

Health and well-being in the workplace have become major concern in contemporary life. These topics continue to dominate the pages of practitioner-oriented magazines. Moe recently such topics are receiving attention in scholarly research journals. For a variety of reasons, these issues occupy a much more prominent niche in mainstream organizational research.

First, an individual's experience at work obviously affects the person while she or he is in theworkplace. In addition, these experiences also "spill over" into non-work domains. Workers almost spend one-third of their waking hours at work, they don't necessarily leave the job behind when they leave the work site. Indeed, the overlap between non-work and wok leads to the observation that a person's work and personal lives are interrelated and interwined. Second, there is a growing awareness that certain elements in the workplace pose risks for workers. Unsafe work practices, sexual harassment, disturbing supervisor-subordinate relationship, and uncontrolled aggression are such potential threats. Third, health problems adversely affect outcomes. Workers experiencing poor health may be less productive, make lower quality decisions, exhibit higher absenteeism and make consistently diminishing overall contributions to the organization.

Figure 1 presents an organizing framework that both guides our discussion and highlights the major elements of the network of health and well-being in the workplace.

Figure 1: An Organizing Framework

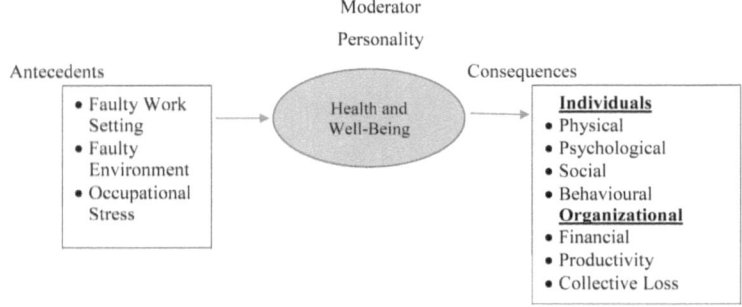

The concept of well-being is seen as the broader and more encompassing construct. Specifically, well-beingisviewed as comprising thevarious life/non-work satisfactions enjoyed by individuals (satisfaction with self, family life, social life, recreation, spirituality, and so forth), work/job-related satisfactions, and general (psychological) well-being. General health/well-being is seen as a state of equilibrium at the physical, mental, social and spiritual domains (World Health Organization).

At the operational level, behavioural scientists have stressed three aspects of the construct definition. First, well-being includes *total life satisfaction*. It provides an overall assessment of person's subjective well-being. Second, well-being denotes "feel good" component. Majority of psychologists view that *frequent experience of moderately positive affects* (emotion) is a more reliable indicator of well-being compared with infrequent experience of strong positive emotions. Third, satisfaction in several domains of life (such as work, family, social relation, and so forth) is also an essential component. A comprensive measure includes an integrated composite index of these three components.

Measurement

Well-being is not a unitary construct. There are several components of subjective well-being (SWB): life satisfaction (global judgment of one's life), satisfaction with important domains (e.g., work satisfaction), positive affect (experiencing many pleasant emotions and moods), and low levels of negative affect (experiencing few unpleasant emotions and moods).

In early research on well-being, researchers studied only a single self-report item for measurement. For example, Andrews and Withey (1976) asked participants about the feeling of life as a whole on 7-point scale ranging from delighted to terrible. Current measure of well-being includes multiple items. For example, the *PANAS (Positive and Negative Affect Scale)* assesses both positive and negative affect, each with ten affect items. The gap score between positive affect experience ratings and negative affect experience rating is indicative of wellness or illness.

In the past, researchers have used additional types of assessment to obtain a better gauge of long-term feelings. One such measure is *Experience Sampling Method (ESP)*. Considering the view that one-time self-report life satisfaction scale is inadequate, ESM measures life satisfaction and memories of positive and negative life events.

On the basis of World Value Survey – II (World Value Survey Group, 1994) three components of well-being have been recognized: life satisfaction, pleasant affect, and unpleasant affect. The life satisfaction score is based on respondents' answers to the question: "all things considered, how satisfied you are with your life these days?" This was used with the help of number from 1 (dissatisfied) to 10 (satisfied). Later many researches have adopted this format, but have usually included multi-item scales.

Other physiological measures, reports by informants, memory and reaction time measures are included inn order to make measurement complete. Though each of these measures has limitation, the merits of different kinds of measures are complementary to each other. For example, in the memory measure, participants are asked to generate as many positive and negative events from their lives as they can during a short span of time. With the help of this method, researchers can measure individual difference in the relative accessibility of memories for good and bad events and structure of respondent's recall of their lives.

Diener argues that the frequency count of intense positive emotion is not proper indication of well-being. He viewed that how much of the time a person experiences well-being is a better predictor than positive emotional intensity of how happy the person reports being. Intense positive moments are rare even among the happiest individuals. Instead, happy individuals report mild-to-moderate pleasant emotions most of the time whether they are alone or with others, at work or in free time.

Predictors of Well-Being

A pertinent area of discussion in the context of well-being involves the identification of predictors (or correlates) of well-being. Some predictors are psychological (internal factors) whereas other factors are external. These internal and external factors either amplify or restrict the quantum of well-being.

Psychological Factors

The psychological factors of well-being include factors such as personality and self-esteem.

Personality. In recent years, a number of studies have examined the role of personality in well-being. The long popular belief is that temperament is more important to well-being than are the number of external blessings.

Personality traits account for a larger portion of variance in individual differences in well-being. Research has shown that certain personality traits are related to well-being. In general, extraverts report being happier that introverts, and neurotics report less happy than emotionally stable individual. The traits of agreeableness and conscientiousness have also been found to be positively elated to well-being.

Self-esteem. Self-esteem has been defined as a global feeling of self-worth or adequacy as a person, or a generalized feeling of self-acceptance and self-respect. Well-being and self-esteem appear to be linked.

Sociodemographic Factors

In addition to psychological factors, a number of sociodemographic predictors need to be identified.

Genetic Factors. The idea of a genetically determined *set point for* well-being is a seminal point. Lykken and Tellegen (1996) have provided evidence based a twin studies and adoption studies. That the heritability of well-being may be as high as 80% (although a more widely accepted figure is 50%). Whatever the exact coefficient, its large magnitude suggests that for each person there is indeed a chronic or characteristic level of well-being. Consistent with this idea, lottery winners and victims of skeletal injuries are found to keep returning to their own baseline over time.

Age. Researchers have found that older people tend to be somewhat happier than younger people. Christensen's (1995) social-emotional sensitivity theory suggests that old people learn to structure their lives and pursue particular goals that maximize positive emotions, consistent with proposition that people can learn to sustainably increase their well-being. Further these age-related increases in well-being are in part mediated by volitional changes including older peoples ability to select moe enjoyable and self-appropriate goals.

While some studies indicate the positive influence of age, at least up to a level of advancing age, other studies found that young people were happier than the old. Youth activities are related to positive developmental changes. Participation in school extracurricular activities and community youth organizations has been found to be correlated with higher self-esteem, feeling of control over one's life, higher educational aspiration and achievement, all together contribute to well-being.

Gender. In general, women are as happy as men are. It is an interesting observation that the range of emotion experienced by women is greater than that of men. Consequently women experience greater depression (negative emotion) compared with men, but women also have greater capacity to experience joy. Hence there is no significant gender difference with respect to well-being.

It is worth noting that men and women handle their emotions in different ways. For example, women report using social support more frequently than men to combat the negative moods. However, the emotional benefits that women gain through affiliation may be undercut by their greater tendency (relative to men) to ruminate about the causes and consequences of their unhappiness.

Income. Income has an effect only at extreme levels of poverty but once the basic needs are met, income is no longer influential. Further factors such as power and statues that co-vary with income may be responsible for the effect of income on well-being.

Unemployment, it is found that unemployment people experience brings less well-being. Unemployment causes unhappiness even when income differences are controlled. However, it does not appear that homemakers are less happy than those who work in salaried jobs. Job satisfaction appears to be related to well-being.

Education. The effects of education on well-being do not appear to be strong. Several studies have found that there is no significant effect. Several studies have indicated more positive effect for women. Campbell's (1981) analysis suggests that although education may serve as a resource for persons, it may also raise aspiration and alert the person to alternative types of life.

Marriage. A number of large scale studies indicate that married persons report greater well-being than unmarried persons. Although married women may report greater stress symptoms than unmarried women, they also report greater satisfaction. Glenn and Weaver (1979) found that marriage was the strongest predictor of well-being when education, income and occupational status are controlled. When one turns from the objective fact of marriage to the importance of marital satisfaction on global well-being, the conclusion is that marriage and family satisfaction is one of the most important predicators of well-being.

Other Relevant Predictors

Apart from psychological and sociodemographic factors, a few other predictors are relevant in the context of well-being.

Social Support. Social support is one of the most effective means by which people cope with stressful events, thereby buffering themselves from the adverse mental and physical health effects of stress. It effectively reduces psychological distress, such as depression and anxiety, during times of stress and is associated with a variety of physical health benefits including positive adjustment.

Spirituality. It is shown that an involvement for searching a meaning and purpose in life, unfolding mysteries of the universe, harmony, peace, wholeness and transcendence is a stable predictor of well-being. Taylor noted that spirituality was superior in predicting positive health outcome for individuals who were not religious. The spiritual well-being mediates the relation between culture, specific coping and quality of life. Individuals higher in spirituality have greater access to spiritual and religious coping resources. Boland (2000) asserts that spirituality allows an individual to draw inner resources that facilitate adaptive coping and positive health outcomes. A number of studies have shown that people's active participation in faith communities significantly contribute towards well-being.

Process Nature of Well-Being

While the identification of predictors of well-being offers scope for increment and decrement of well-being, a search for theoretical framework has generated many useful ideas to understand the process nature of well-being. These ideas can appropriately be used for wellness enhancement program.

It is believed that there are three primary types of factors that affect well-being namely, the set point, life circumstances, and the individual. Existing evidence suggests that genetics account for approximately 50% of the population variation and circumstances account for approximately 10%. This leaves as much as 40% of that variance. Now the fundamental question concerns as to the source of this 40%. A number of viable explanatory solutions have been offered.

Intentional Activity

Lyubomirsky and her colleagues offer evidence suggesting that volitional efforts (intentional activity) offer a route to longitudinal increases in well-being. According to Lyubomirsky, individuals are very active creatures, with innumerable behaviours, projects and concerns to which that devote energy. Intentional activity refers to volitional efforts. It assumes that intentional activities require some degree of effort to enact. There is a critical distinction between the category of activity and category of life circumstances. Circumstances happen to people, and activities are ways that people act on circumstances. Thus, intentional activity influences well-being. For example, some types of behavioural activity, such as exercising regularly or trying to be kind to others, are associated with well-being.

Telic Theories

Telic or end-point theories maintain that well-being is gained when some state, such as goal, need, is reached. It is maintained that satisfaction of needs causes wellness and conversely, the persistence of unfulfilled needs causes unhappiness.

Alternatively telic theories derive from different origins of the strivings. In need theories, there are certain innate or learned needs that the person seeks to fulfill. The person may or may not be aware of these needs. Nevertheless, it is postulated that well-being will follow from their fulfillment. In contrast, goal theories are based on specific desires of which the person is aware. The person is consciously seeking certain goals and well-being results when they are reached. Goals and needs are related in that underlying needs may lead to specific goals. Needs may universal, such as those postulated by Maslow or they may differ from individual to individual.

Top-Down versus Bottom-Up Theories

Bottom-up theories maintain that well-being is simply the sum of many small pleasures. According to this view, when a person judges whether his or her life is happy some mental calculation is used to sum the momentary pleasure and pain. A happy life in this view is an accumulation of happy moments. In contrast, the top-down approach assumes that there is a global propensity to experience things in a positive way and this propensity influences that momentary world. In other words, a person enjoys pleasure because he or she is happy, not vice versa.

Associationistic Theories

Many theories are based on memory, conditioning or cognitive principles that can be subsumed under the broad rubric of associationistic models. Cognitive approaches to well-being are in their infancy. Onecognitive approach rests on the attributions (explanations) people make about the events happening to them. For example, those events bring the most well-being if they are attributed to internal stable factors.

One general cognition approach to well-being has to do with associative networks in memory. Bower (1981) has shown that people will recall memories that are affectively congruent with their current emotional state. Research on memory network suggests that persons could develop a rich network of positive associations and a more limited and isolated network of negative ones. In such persons, more events or ideas could be happy ideas and affect. Thus, a person with such a predominantly positive network could be predisposed to react to more events in a positive way.

A related type to theory is based on classically conditioned elicitation of affect. Research has shown that affective conditioning can be extremely resistant to extinctions. Thus, happy persons might be those who have had very positive affective experiences associated with a large number of frequent every day stimuli Zajonc' (1980) contends that affective reaction occurs independently or/and more rapidly than cognitive evaluation of stimuli.

There is some evidence that a person can give conscious directions to the affective association in his or her life. Fordyce (1977) offered evidence that a conscious attempt to reduce negative thoughts can increase happiness. Kamman (1982) found that reciting positive statements in the morning leads to a happier day. Goodhart has found that positive thinking similar to that recommended by Norman Peale is correlated with well-being. Thus, explicit conscious attempt to avoid negative thoughts and to think of happy ones may increase happiness.

Certain individuals may have built up a strong network of positive associations and learned to react habitually in a positive way. These individuals are characterized as possessing a happy temperament. A person with a Pollyanna approach to life is perhaps the prototype of a person who has formed positive associations to the world. Several studies have found a relationship between happiness, a cognitive bias towards positive associations and high Pollyanna personality scores.

Judgment Theories

Judgment theories maintain that well-being results from a comparison between some standard and actual conditions. It actual conditions exceed, happiness will result. In the case of satisfaction, such comparisons may be conscious. However, in the case of affect, comparison with a standard may occur in a nonconscious manner.

Judgment theories are classified on the basis of the standard that is used. In social comparison theories, one uses other people as a standard. If a person is better off than others, persons would be satisfied or happy. Sometimes a person's past life is used to set standard. It the individual's current life exceeds this standard, that person will probably be happy.

In social comparison framework, proximal others are usually weighted heavily because of their salience. Will (1981) showed that downward comparison with less fortunate persons can increase well-being. Kearle (1981) found that believing others live in poor circumstances can enhance one's life satisfaction. It is argued that whether the amount of income that will satisfy people depends on the income of others in the society. One shortcoming to social comparison theories is that they do not make clear when a person will need to make comparison with others.

Adaption theory is based on a standard derived from an individual's own experience. If current events are better than the standard, the individuals will be happy. However, if the good events continue, adaptation will occur, the individual's standard will rise, so that it eventually matches the newer events. Thus, according to the adaptation theory, recent changes produce happiness and unhappiness because a person will eventually adapt to the overall level of events. It is shown that lottery winners are no happier and quadriplegics a less happy than normal control. It is suggested that people adapt to all events, no matter how fortunate or unfortunate. It is also found that spinal cord injury victims are extremely unhappy after their accidents. However, their affect quickly begins moving back towards happiness suggesting that adaptation is occurring rapidly even to this extreme misfortune.

One popular form of judgment theory is aspiration level. It maintains that happiness will depend on the discrepancy in a person's life between actual conditions and aspirations. Happiness depends on the ratio of unfulfilled desires to total desires. According to this theory, high aspirations are as much a threat to happiness as are bad conditions. The level of aspiration presumely comes from an individual's previous experience, goals and so forth. Although there is evidence that supports the idea that the discrepancy between actual conditions and the level a person aspires is correlated with well-being, this relationship does not appear to be strong.

Workplace Well-Being

While the conceptualization of health and well-being tends to be a broad and encompassing concept involving the whole person, organizational research has included both generalized job-elated experiences (job satisfaction, job attachment) as well as more domain-specific dimensions (satisfaction with pay). The pertinent literature in the area has identified three areas of concerns: **antecedent factors, personality factors,** and **outcome factors.**

Antecedent Factors

A number of antecedent factors such as hazardous setting, over-staffing, excessive over-time, rapid implementation and change of technology pose threats.

Personality Factors

Personality A (Type A Behaviour Pattern) denoting time urgency, moderate level of aggressiveness and striving for accomplishment is a stressor. Specifically hostility in employees is a risk factor.

Role-related Stressors

A number of role-related stressors (role overload, role ambiguity, role expectation, inter-role conflict and role stagnation) complicate stress scenarios. Udai Pareek's work and tips offer very helpful solutions.

Appendix
The Life Orientation Scale (LOS)
F M Sahoo

Part – 1

Instruction

Below are ten statements that you may agree or disagree. Using the 1-7 scale, please indicate the amount of your agreement or disagreement with each item by placing the appropriate number on the line beside that item. Please be open and honest in your response.

1. Strongly disagree
2. Disagree
3. Slightly disagree
4. **Neither agree nor disagree**
5. Slightly agree
6. Agree
7. Strongly agree

The life I live is close to my ideal.
I enjoy the respect I am given.
My family members would describe me as satisfied.
I wish I had more respect given to me.
I am pleased with the way I have fulfilled my duties.
I wish I were more at peace.
If I could live my life once again, I would want it to be almost exactly the same.
I feel good about my life.
My family members approve of my life.
I feel at peace.

Part -2
Instruction

As an individual, you have several areas of your activity. Listed are such domains. Examine your feeling in each of these domains. Consider your feeling and experiences and indicate the degree of satisfaction with each of these domains. Put a number from 1 to 7 where "1" represents "terrible" feeling '7' represents "delightful" feeling.

- **Education (of self or children)**
- Coaching
- Exam Performance
- Teachers
- School environment
- College environment
- **Social Relation**
- Neighbours
- Friends
- Colleagues
- Visitors
- **Self in general**
- Physical health
- Achievement
- Morality (ethical)
- **Recreation**
- Games and Sports
- Social get-together
- Hobbies
- TV/Movies
- **Work**
- Pay
- Boss

- Physical surrounding
- **Finance**
- Income
- Expenditure
- Investment
- Debt
- **Family**
- Spouse
- Children
- Relatives
- Daily Living

Part-3

Instruction

Reflect on your experience for last two months and indicate the degree you have been experiencing each of these mental states. Using the 1-5 scale, indicate the number to express the intensity of your experience.

1. Never
2. Rarely
3. Sometimes
4. Often
5. Almost always

Cheerful	Depressed
Irritable	Lively
Happy	Gloomy
Joyful	Spirited
Nervous	Energetic
Scared	
Lonely	
Sad	Disgusted
Delighted	Optimistic
Shaky	Relaxed

Tired   Withdrawn
Excited   Enthusiastic
Alert   Dissatisfied

Part-4
Instruction

Please indicate this personal information.

Name (optional):
Sex:
Age:
Residence:
Occupation:
Income (Monthly):
Education

    Thank you for your cooperation

Scoring Notes

The scoring isself-explanatory. Part 1 itemscore keyed in positive directions excepting 4th and 6th items which are to be reverse-scored. Sum of scores across ten items is indicative of total life satisfaction. For Part 2, domain-specific satisfaction can be determined in terms of general satisfaction and specific satisfaction. For example, the rating for education is the general satisfaction with education. The ratings given for coaching, exam, etc. can be added across these sub-items. The average of these summed rating denotes specific satisfaction with education. For Part 3, positive affect score can be computed by adding ratings across 12 positive items. Similarly, negative affect score can be determined. The difference of these two scores is indicative of PANAS score. This is indicative of happiness / unhappiness.

Note: The LOS has been taken from F.M. Sahoo, et. al's Book *Happiness Flows*

PART-2
SUPPLEMENTARY READINGS

Chapter 12

Creativity

Marks of creation are effective dividers between ages. A creative literary movement separates one period from the other in literature. A creative trend in painting leaves indelible marks for distinguishing one period from the other in art. The creative scientific achievement marks the beginning of a new era in science. Although historians use events as bases for labeling historical periods, they essentially choose events that have characteristics of creativity.

Although creativity is seminal, it has not received research attention proportional to its utility in our lives. It was only J.P. Guilford (1950) who made a fervent appeal for research on creativity. In 1950, Guilford was elected as the President of the American Psychological Association and his presidential address was titled *creativity*. In fact, his research article provided impetus to subsequent works on the problem of creativity.

Guilford's (1950) early work served two important purposes. First, it provided an operational definition of creativity. Second, it explicated the process nature of creativity by specifying interactive components such as content, process and the product. Guilford received the American Psychological Association's Distinguished Contribution Award for his seminal work.

It is generally agreed that creative products are novel and useful. It is novel in the sense that it is original. Since original or novel products are not ordinarily expected, these products generate surprisingness. However, all unusual and uncommon products are not considered creative. The products must be having utility factor. The delirium of a madman may be uncommon, but it is not regarded as a creative product.

In addition to originality, the other indices of creativity were also identified. These include fluency, flexibility and elaboration. These parameters are explicit when specific tests of creativity are considered. A classic illustration involves Guilford's Usual Unusual Test. The test requires individuals to indicate multiple uses of an usual thing. When used for children, the test requires children to indicate several ways of using a piece of brick. In this case, the child may provide such an answer: brick can be used to construct a house, a temple, a store, an office and a school. However, another child may offer a different answer: brick can be used to construct a house: brick can be used as a paper weight: brick can be used to write something on a wall; brick can be used to drive away a cat: brick can be used as a door block.

The analysis of the responses of these two children reveals the difference. Fluency refers to the amount of ideas generated per unit time. Since both of these children have produced five ideas, each should get the credit of 5 marks for fluency. Flexibility defines the number of thought categories. The first child has produced ideas that belong to the single category of "construction". On the contrary, the second child has offered ideas belonging to five separate categories. Consequently, the first child is entitled to a score of 1 whereas the second child is entitled to a score of 5 with respect to flexibility. Originality is not difficult to quantity. If a large number of children are asked the same question, the statistical computation can be made with respect to the unusualness of a particular response. Greater is the unusualness, higher is the originality score. The creativity indices (**fluency, flexibility and originality**) produce test scores separately; these scores can be summed to generate an overall creativity score. In many domains such as science and literature, the person has to elaborate the creative ideas produced. The elaboration gives out implication and inputs for evaluation.

A representative sample of tests of creativity are likely to offer ideas that are helpful for evaluating the psychometric approach. One such test involves Flanagan's Ingenuity Test. This requires subjects to offer insightful solutions for certain social problems. Guilford's Consequences. Test is also an oft-used measure. It requires respondents to imagine the consequences of some unusual happenings. Children may be asked to indicate consequences in the context of several hypothetical situations. They are asked to tell what would happen if schools have wheels. What would happen if lions could speak? What would happen if humans would not require food? What would happen if birds could talk? Getzels and Jackson suggested a test called Fable Ending. Children are asked to read an incomplete fable. They are asked to complete it by adding themes. The analysis of the inclusion reveals creativity of children. Similarly, the Plot Title Test requires children to provide a little for a short story. Torrance popularized Project Improvement Test. Children are given a material such as a toy car. They are asked to improvise it. All these tests generate responses that can be scored in terms of fluency, flexibility and originality.

During the 1950s and 1960s, the basic approach in the field of creativity was essentially a psychometric orientation. Children and adults were tested on creativity and creative individuals were identified. The objective of such measurements was to identify the creative individuals and to expose then to creativity training programme.

The creativity training programmes essentially involve the stimulation of divergent thinking. It was postulated that divergent thinking is the process variable in creativity. As has been illustrated, the child indicating the flexibility of thought responds divergently. On the contrary the child replying in terms of a single thought category such as constructing a house and a constructing a school gives evidence of convergent thinking. Since divergent thinking was thought to underlie the creative process, the training programmes gravitated towards the development of divergent thinking style.

Training for Creativity

During war periods, a number of psychologists attempted to formulate specific training programme that would stimulate creativity. Osborn devised and popularized a method called *brainstorming*. It was argued that the method of brainstorming would be very helpful in stimulating creativity in individuals. It would provide a situation where individuals should be prompted to generate creative solutions. The method is basically used in a group context. A problem is posed and individuals are encouraged to generate solutions. The process consists of two sequential stages: green light stage and red light stage.

The first phase of the brainstorming is labeled green light stage. This is an evaluation-free stage where participating individuals are encouraged to suggest all possible solutions. Assurances are given that no answer would be subjected to criticism and evaluation. People should present as many solutions as possible. They should not be hesitant to offer remote and far-fetched solutions. For instance, children may be asked to suggest the method of preparing a cup of tea. A child may offer a very unusual answer in terms of pouring the milk from the roof top. The child may add that a pot placed on the stove on the ground would prepare the tea. Apparently this solution is a ridicules one. However, the climate of the training session is shaped in such a fashion that the solutions are not rejected at the first instance. It is called brainstorming because there is total freedom on the expression of the thoughts that are crowding a participant's mind.

However, the brainstorming slowly switches over to a second phase called red light stage. All the solutions are considered one by one. Solutions are evaluated in terms of certain specific criteria such as desirability and feasibility. Naturally the quality solutions are identified and selected.

The past research has shown that brainstorming is successful in inculcating creative orientation in participants. The method has been extensively used in decision making sessions of managers in organization. This has also been used to stimulate creativity in children. Sometimes, the criticism is leveled that some participants may feel hesitant to express their ideas because of the contradictory solution offered by their revered persons. With a view to getting around this problem, the modern practice is to use *electronic brainstorming.* In electronic brainstorming each of the participants is provided with a computer terminal where he or she enters his or her ideas. Since the ideas are simultaneously pooled, there is no apprehension that a person's response would inhibit another individual. However, the red light stage evaluates all the solutions generated in this process.

Another training method is based on the similar concept of analogical thinking which is considered central to the creative process. The divergent thinking has sometimes been termed *remote association*. Poincare, the celebrated nuclear mathematician, remarks that creativity is a process of establishing intimacy between two or more strange ideas. In other words, a creative person discovers some form of similarity between two or more dissimilar ideas or objects.

With this rationale, the **method of *synectics*** is used. This method encourages participants to imagine similarity between themselves and some other objects. For instance, participants are encouraged to contemplate similarities with other objects and living beings. It may take the form of *direct analogy*. The person is encouraged to imagine similarities between two or more apparently different objects or animals. Graham Bell, the inventor of telephone, thought of the similarity between the membrane in the inner ear and wire. He reasoned that if the soft membrane could cause vibration in the bone, it would be possible for the wire to cause vibration producing sound. This gave rise to the invention of Bell's telephone system.

Another form of analogy involves *personal analogy*. The participants in synectics are asked to imagine themselves as other objects or living beings. It is important to indicate that the chemist Kekul was pondering over the molecular structure of Benzine. He dreamt of a snake holding it's tall in its mouth. This was helpful in solving his problem.

Similarity, participants are trained to develop *biological analogy*. They are asked to imagine themselves as different parts of a human body. They may also be asked to imagine themselves as other living beings or any limb of other beings. Thus, people are trained to stretch their imagination, shed inhibitions and use *fantasy*. It is assumed that an extended use of analogical *thinking* paves the way for creative process.

More recently, Steinberg and his associates have popularized another technique called *"thinking hats"*. In the training session, hats of different colours are used. The entire group is randomly divided into a small number of subgroups. Members of each subgroup put on caps of a particular colour. Then a problem is presented. Members wearing blue hats are asked to solve the problem by analytical method whereas members wearing red hats are asked to solve it by employing synthetic method. In essence, different groups are asked to solve problem by using different methods. Following the solution of the problem, hats are exchanged. Now a subgroup attempts solution by using different procedure. Thus, participants are trained to free themselves from the fixed pattern of problem solving style.

The Creative Process

Although these training methods have varied degree of success, a better understanding of creativity involves the analysis of creative process. As pointed out earlier, many psychologists have stressed **divergent thinking** in creative process. The divergent thinking is exemplified by a child's divergent answer to the question. How can you use a piece of brick? The answer in terms of using the brick to build a house, to write something on the wall, to use it as a paperweight, and so on. It is indicative of divergent thought, as thought categories do not converge on a single point. However, emphasis on divergent thinking raises a fundamental question. Is convergent thinking unrelated to creative process?

Kuhn (1966) offers an interesting answer Kuhn was originally a physicist, but later developed interest in the study of the history of behavioural and social sciences. His study gave him an insight. His concept of *paradigm crisis* has become a standard reference in the philosophy of science. He observed that it is unlikely to meet Mr. Novelty if a person makes random wanderings. It is better to concentrate on normative practices and methods initially. If a person follows established practices and methods, it is also likely that some deviate cases would be encountered. It the person considers this deviate case seriously, novel method and product would emerge.

Kuhn (1966) offers several example. For instance, at one point of time people considered the shape of the earth as a flat surface. They were carrying out navigation. Things were going well till a point when their computation decided one destination but they actually arrived in a different place. This generated what Kuhn calls *essential tension*. The paradigm crisis causes tension and the solution leads to *paradigm shift*. Kuhn adds that paradigm crisis and its resulting paradigm shift have brought about major breakthrough in scientific and creative thought. In this process Kepller was outdated by Newton; Newton's laws were again eclipsed by laws of quantum-physics. Newton's laws were alright so far as objects were concerned. But these were rendered inapplicable when subatomic particles were thought upon.

In other words, Kuhn stressed the cycle of convergent and divergent thought process. Initially convergent thinking may be necessary. But an encounter with a deviate case needs to trigger divergent thinking. Fleming's invention of penicillin is an exemplary case. Fleming was conducting bacteria culture. One-day Fleming observed that all the bacterias on the pot had been destroyed and there was fungus formation. Ordinarily Fleming would have dismissed the case with the consideration that it was a faulty experimentation. He would have repeated the experiment again. But Fleming pondered over the cause of fungus formation. This gave rise to the invention of life-saving drug of penicillin. Thus, convergent and divergent skills seem to be necessary at different phases.

Phases of Creative Process

In order to specify phases where divergent thinking is preferable to convergent thinking, psychologists have conceptualized *four stages* of creative thinking. These include: preparation, exploration, incubation, and evaluation.

Preparation. The first stage of creative process is designated as the preparation. The individual sets his or her goal and arranges preliminary materials irrespective of the domain of creativity, the person has to have goal clarity. Scientists must know what they are looking for. At this stage convergent thinking is helpful. The convergent thinking is known as vertical thinking. It is comparable to the process of digging a specific place intensively, whereas divergent thinking is comparable to the activity of digging several places. Needless to say, convergent thinking is effective in delineating the main goal and specific subgoals. The problem must be properly identified.

Exploration During the phase of exploration, the creative activity takes a different form. An active exploration reflects divergent thinking. In this phase, there are two important characteristics. First, there is a remarkable difference between a coping personality and a creative personality. For solution of the problem at hand, individuals with creative personalities search for alternatives by making use of divergent thinking. However, copers select alternative on the basis of learning experience. They select the alternatives that have been rewarded in the past. The creative person, on the other hand, selects alternatives on the basis of novelty and surprisingness. The unusual and original alternatives that are likely to generate surprisingness are selected. Thus, a poet selects diction that would surprise readers. A painter selects the colour that would move a critic. It is important to recognize that an intense form of divergent thinking facilitates successful exploration.

Incubation. This is a period of no apparent overt activity. It is quite possible that the artist or the scientist is either unable to solve the problem or he/she is not fully satisfied with the obtained outcome. The task remains unfinished. In such a situation, they abandon the search process temporarily and get themselves engaged with other pursuits.

Although this is a period of no overt activity in the domain of specific creative area, it cannot be designated as a period of vacuum. In the absence of conscious efforts, the person incubates and continues with it at the subconscious and unconscious levels. While they are busy in performing their day-to-day activity, the latent thought content is centered on problem solution. In a number of cases, the solution is achieved during this incubation period.

Everyone is familiar with the case of Archimedes who got the insight while taking bath in his home. His euphoric Eureka (I have got it) is a vivid illustration of problem-solving in an incubation phase.Recently the world-famous mathematician, Poincare, has indicated an evidence. Despite much effort, he could not solve a mathematical function. Then he gave up and went on a geological tour. As he was getting into a bus during his tour, the geometric pattern of the climbing steps gave him an instant insight. He came home and solved the problem.

Many creative persons have stressed the role of unconscious process in creativity. They have explicated as to how certain novel and bright ideas surfaced during a dreamlike state. Poet S. T. Coleridge, speaks of his composition of the famous poem *Kubla Khan*. The three hundred line poem took its form when he was asleep.

Evaluation. The last and fourth stage of creative process is designated evaluation. Having solved the problem, creative persons elaborate the ideas. They think about its implications. More importantly, they evaluate the creative product prior to its dissemination. A poet reads out his poem before his or her spouse, close relatives, intimate associates, and a few chosen readers. The poet also considers possible reception at the end of critics. Needless to say, this process of examination and evaluation entails convergent thinking.

Thus, the analysis of the creative process is linked with stages of creativity. It is clearly shown that creative process requires the cycle of convergent-divergent-convergent thought process. The preparation starts with convergent thinking whereas exploration is based on divergent thinking. Convergent thinking is again repeated at the evaluation phase. Compared to scientific creativity, the cycle has to be repeated a greater number of times in artistic and literary creativity.

Relevant Factors

During the creative process, the relevance of certain specific factors has been identified. Creative persons have spoken about the role of inspiration in their work. The Greek poets describe how divinity inspired them to write poems. Indian poets in the past have admitted the role of divine inspiration. British poet Blake spoke of many mystical experiences in his life. It is quite plausible that the justification of inspiration is surely a manifestation of their *self-motivation.*

Contemporary research on creativity clearly redefines "talent" Renzuli offers a graphic description. According to Renzulli, there are three clusters (motivation, intelligence, and creativity) which overlap each other. This pictorial representation depicts several types. Some people have only one of these three attributes.

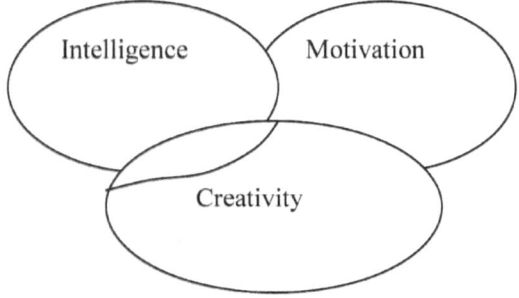

For instance, they may have creativity but it is devoid of motivation and intelligence. Without motivation, it does not last for long; without intelligence, it does not reach high level. Similarly we would expect people who have two of these attributes. For example, with intelligence and creativity, people can generate creative idea, but the lack of hard work does not give it a tangible form. On the contrary, a small number of people possess all these three attributes. Needless to say, their motivation, intelligence and creative ability bring out the creative products on a lasting and tangible manner.

At this point, it is logical to comment on the relationship between intelligence and creativity. Empirical studies examining this relationship has indicated low positive correlation between the two. It implies that all creative individuals have moderate to high intelligence. But all intelligent persons are not creative. It appears that intelligence functions as a threshold for creative activity but it does not predict creativity beyond certain level.

More recently, the significance of emotional intelligence has been highlighted. Of course the role of self-motivation implicitly signals the value of emotional intelligence. The word "emotion" is also derived from the fact that it enhances motion (motivation). It appears plausible that emotion in general and emotional intelligence in particular accelerates the creative process. This view is consistent with the contemporary recognition that human brain has two distinct structures "feeling brain" and "thinking brain". Furthermore, from evolutionary point of view, feeling brain is older than the thinking brain.

The Theoretical Position

In view of these recent evidence relating to creative process, contemporary theorists offer an component analysis of creative process. According to Amabile (2001), major components of creative process include domain-relevant skills, the creativity-related process and intrinsic task-relevant involvement. The domain-relevant skills, according to this component analysis, comprise cognitions and abilities which Guilford termed talent in 1958. Included are also acquired learning and skills. The creativity-related process involve personalities and work habits to be discussed later. Finally, the intrinsic task-relevant motivation is characterized by interest, enjoyment, satisfaction and challenge of the work. Although creative persons are motivated by external reward conditions such as prizes and recognition during the preparatory phase (first ten/fifteen years), these external awards lose importance for them as they advance.

Steinberg (2001) uses another expression *resources theory* for the components of creativity. Although Steinberg lists cognitive resources, motivational resources and environmental resources, there is no major difference from components analysis. In component analysis, the creativity-relevant process includes not only intra-individual factors such as personality and work habits it also includes extra-individual factors such as social environment.

Steinberg has further specified the components in a new rubric termed *confluence theory*. Creativity is a confluence of six basic elements such as intelligence, cognitions, personality, thinking style, intrinsic motivation and supportive environment. Although a common man with some of these resources can exhibit mundane creativity – the kind of creativity we come across day-to-day life – these resources are needed for *exceptional creativity*. Similarly some creative persons exhibit creativity within the normative practices of the society. This is boundary-touching creativity. On the contrary, a few other creative persons present products which contradict existing norms. This is called *boundary breaking creativity*.

The Creative Person

A comprehensive understanding of the creative process is incomplete without explication of person-relevant factors. In the past, the research on creativity basically adopted psychometric methods. Children and persons were classified into creative and non-creative on the basis of standardized test scores; comparison of groups revealed certain information. However, a more dynamic method called *evolving system approach* (ESA) has been adopted during last two decades. This system involves an intensive study of the life histories and life span development of creative personalities. In this process, the personal notes, writings, diaries, and activities of creative scientists like Darwin, Linus Pauling and Thomas Young have been examined. Similarly, observations have been made with respect to the noted authors like John Irving and Donaldson and Painter Monet. The ESA method has provided wealthful information.

The person variables associated with the creative process include studies of intelligence, cognitive style, personality, psychopathology and development spurts.

Intelligence. Many investigators have been interested in the extent to which creativity requires superior intelligence. Using performance on standard IQ tests as the gauge of intellectual capacity, the early research indicated that a certain threshold-level of intelligence was required for the manifestation of creativity, but that beyond that threshold, intelligence bore a minimal relation with creative behaviour. As pointed out earlier, Renzulli's concept of three overlapping clusters of abilities (creative ability, motivational ability and intellectual ability) provides a better conceptualization of creative person. A creative person, in this scheme, is considered as one having all three clusters of abilities whereas other persons do possess none of these abilities, or two of these abilities or one of these abilities. More critical is the realization that simplistic, exclusive and unidimensional concept of intelligence is to be replaced by a more complex, inclusive and multidimensional constructs. Examples are Guilford's structure of intellect model, Steinberg's triatchic theory of intelligence, and Gardener's multiple theory of intelligence. The last theory is especially provocative in the sense that it includes abilities which are not a part of standard psychometric tests (e.g., musical, bodily-kinesthetic, interpersonal and intrapersonal intelligence). Moreover, each intelligence is associated with a specific manifestation of creativity, such as painting, choreography or psychology.

Cognitive Style. As indicated earlier, creativity involves analogical thinking. Sometimes this is called "remote association". Studies using evolving system approach offer some useful information regarding the evolution of creative product. For instance, a close examination of writings of Stephen Donaldson suggests a geneplore model of relative cognition.

According to this model, the creative person explores and generates a large number of ideas. Some ideas take the form of candidates for creative work. This "preinventive form" is used for further exploration. While screening pre-inventive types, the person adopts the criteria of novelty, surprisingness, and aesthetics. This is followed by a process of combinations. Combinations generate new cognitions. The convergence of discrepant ideas become the hallmark of creativity.

Creative-ideas can always be analysed into perception of an analogy between old ideas, previously thought to be strangers to one another. Thus, capacity for analogical thinking is necessary for creative inspiration. Thomas Young, the noted physicist, linguist and psychologist, propounded his wave theory of light on the basis of this insightful observation of waves of water. Darwin's constant use of the metaphor of "tree of life" reflects his analogical thinking in conceptualizing multilinear evolution of living organisms. However, the insightful problem solving and analogical thinking styles are product of the interaction between creative persons and supportive environment. Although there is some evidence of innate cognitions, expertise acquisition has been clearly shown in the evolving system approach.

Personality. Many researchers have attempted to generate personality profile of a creative person. The first and foremost is the habit of hardwork. Edison categorically asserted "Genius is ninety-nine per cent perspiration, only one-percent inspiration". More recently, the noted American novelist, John Irving has said that seven-eighth portion of his success is a product of hardwork, one-eighth a product of inspiration. During formative years of creative work, the creative persons spend almost ten hours a day.

The other personality traits include high self-confidence, autonomy and independence, wide range of interests, love of novelty and distaste for traditional dogmas, greater openness to new experiences, a more conspicuous behavioural and cognitive flexibility, risk-tasking behaviour .Particularly interesting is what the research has concluded to the longstanding "mad-genius" controversy. These is now significant evidence showing that creativity tends to be associated with certain amount of psychopathology (Eysenck, 1993) At the same time, this association is not equivalent to the claim that creative individuals must necessarily suffer from mental disorders. On the contrary, research has shown that (a) numerous creators have no apparent tendencies towards psychopathology, (b) the incidence varies according to the domain of creative activity, (c) many creators who seemingly exhibit disorders possess compensatory characteristics that enable them to control and sublimate abnormality, and (d) some apparent disorders may be quite adaptive to the creative process in the life of the creators.

Life Span Development. Developmental psychologists have examined longitudinal transformation in creative persons. Broadly, two issues have been addressed. The first one involves the study of early experiences during childhood and adolescence. The second one involves the actualisation of creative potential during adulthood and later years.

It has been shown that certain elements of early years influence creative potential. The birth order, parental loss, marginality and challenging experiences are important ones. An interesting finding in this context shows that creativity does not spring from the highly nurturing home. Rather diversity of experiences, challenging situations and adversity generate perseverance and resilience in creative children. These difficulties trigger efforts to master the environment.

The actualization of creative potential has been studied from developmental perspective. Psychologists have considered creativity as a function of age during adult and old age. Previous research indicated a curvilinear (inverted backward) function. This implies that creativity declines during old age. However, recent evidence does not fully support this conclusion. It is likely that elderly and old people use several compensatory mechanisms. The continuation of vigorous activity may prevent the decline of creative process. The possibility of resurgence of creativity during old age presents an optimistic picture. Furthermore, cognitive aging for Indian population seems to be slower. Although there is no empirical study to show the age-wise creativity in Indian context, the existing hunch favours an optimistic view of elderly persons' creative spurts.

The discussion on creative process entails the role of socio cultural milieu in which creative persons grow, blossom and disseminate their contributions.

The Creative Environment

The original research on creativity tended to adopt an exclusively intra individualistic perspective. Creativity was viewed as a process that took place in the mind of a single individual who possesses the appropriate personal characteristics and developmental experiences. Beginning in the 1970s, more psychologists began to recognize that creativity takes place in a social context. These investigators have looked into the diversity of external conditions including interpersonal environment and disciplinary environment.

Interpersonal Environment. Although there has long existed the popular image of the lone genius, it is clear that much creativity takes place in interpersonal setting. The particular nature of the interpersonal experiences may serve to either enhance or inhibit the amount of creativity shown by the individual. A good illustration of the possibilities may be found in the research of Amabile and her associates on the repercussions of rewards, evaluations, surveillance, and other circumstances. Particularly, valuable is the impact of intrinsic and extrinsic incentives for performing a task. Creativity usually appears more favoured when individuals perform a task for internal enjoyment. However, rewards and external incentives may be useful at times especially during initial phase of creative work.

Disciplinary Environment. Most creators do

not function in isolation. Creativity requires dynamic interaction between three sub-systems, one of which entails the individual creator. The second subsystem is the domain which consists of the set of rules, the repertoire of techniques, and any other abstract attribute that define a particular mode of creativity. The third sub-system is the field, which consists of those persons who work within the same domain, and thus have their creativity governed by the same domain-specific guidelines. These colleagues are essential to the realization of individual creativity, according to systems view. It is because creativity does not exist, until those making up the field declare that the work represents an original contribution.

Sociocultural Environment. The larger sociocultural environment influences the process of creativity. It has become increasingly clear that certain political environment affects the degree of creativity manifested by the corresponding population. Some of these-political influences operate directly on the adult creators, such as when workforce depresses the output. Other political effects function during the developmental stage of an individual's life, either encouraging or discouraging the creative potential. Many nations have experienced golden ages after winning independence from foreign rule with ancient Greece providing a classic example. It is plausible that nationalistic rebellion encourages cultural heterogeneity rather than homogeneity. Cultural diversity seems to facilitate creative process. However, analysis of the sociocultural milieu is only part of the story. For example, the general milieu may explain why the Renaissance began in Italy, but it can not explain why Michelangelo towered over his Italian contemporaries.

Conclusion

Psychologists have registered tremendous progress in the understanding of creative process. The initial notions in the 1950s and 1960s, were centered on the intra-individual processes. Following a lull in the 1970s, research in the 1980s, or 1999s have identified many relevant factors and has stressed interactive position. Furthermore, evolving system approach has offered many insights that were not available by using only psychometric method. However, a number of issues remain unattended. It seem logical that creativity research requires techniques that are really "creative".

Chapter 13

Harnessing the Science of Emotion

Emotions have served adaptive functions throughout human history. Emotional processes that facilitate inter individual bonds (participation in group living) have selective advantage. In recent years, psychological and neuropsychological research has offered substantial amount of guideline for application in life.

Landmarks in Emotion Research

The role of emotion in human functioning has been clarified by certain biopsychological investigations of emotion. There are a couple of landmarks in this context.

In 1848, Phineas Gage, a 25-year-old construction foreman for the Burlington Railroad (USA), was the victim of a tragic accident. In order to lay new tracks, the terrain has to be leveled and Gage was in charge of blasting. On the fateful day, the gunpowder exploded prematurely. Although Gage survived the accident, but he survived it a changed man. Before the accident, Gage had been a responsible, intelligent, socially well-adapted person. Once recovered, he appeared to be as able-bodied as before, but his personality and emotional life had totally changed. Gage became irreverent and impulsive; his abundant profanity offended many. He became unpredictable and undependable. He lost his job and was never again able to hold a responsible position. Later Gage's skull was studied. It was apparent that the damage to Gage's brain affected both *medial prefrontal lobes*, which are involved in planning and emotion.

Drawing on the case analysis of Gage and a few others, it can be suggested that vital functions such as memory, planning and decision-making are localized in the frontal lobe (portion just behind the forehead). **The involvement of the frontal brain in planning and emotion is a seminal idea**.

In 1937, it was found that emotional expression is controlled by several interconnected neural structures called *limbic system*. It is a collection of nuclei and tracts that borders the thalamus (limbic means "border").

More specifically a specific part of limbic system, amygdala, plays a critical role in emotion. In 1939, Kluver and Bucy found a striking *syndrome* (pattern of behaviour) in monkeys that had their *amygdala* removed. The syndrome, known as *Kluver-Bucy syndrome*, includes the following behaviour: the consumption almost anything that is edible, increased sexual activity often directed at inappropriate objects, a tendency to repeatedly investigate familiar objects, and a lack of fear. **Kluver-Bucy syndrome** appears to result from amygdala damage. It is observed in several species.

A human case of Kluver-Bucy syndrome was demonstrated in a tragic way. A human patient with a brain infection exhibited a flat affect. Although originally restless, he ultimately became placid. He appeared indifferent to people or situations. He spent much time gazing at the television, but never learned to turn it on, when the set

was off. He tended to watch reflections of others in the room on the glass screen. He smiled inappropriately and mimicked the gestures and actions of others. Once initiating an imitative series, he would perseverate copying all movements made by another for extended period of time . .
. . . . He engaged in oral exploration of all objects within his grasp. He appeared unable to gain information by tactile or visual means. All objects he could lift were placed on his mouth and sucked or chewed.

Although heterosexual prior to his illness, he was observed in hospital to make advances towards other male patients. He never made advances towards women. Later it was discovered the symptoms appeared to result from amygdala damage.

The landmarks in emotion research provide foundational strength. Later the science evolved more vigorously. Neuroscientists and neuropsychologists conducted experiments that shed considerable light on the way emotions function. This research shows that emotions are governed by **basic principles that can be taught, learned, and applied**. By understanding these principles and making use of their applications, people can bring happiness and flourishing to their lives.

1. **THE PRINCIPLE OF**
Negativity Bias:
> *In the moments of experience, a bad outcome, such as losing Rs1000, feels more extremes and revets more attention than does a comparably good outcome, such as gaining Rs 1000.*

THE APPLICATION:
> *Be aware of this asymmetry. Since negative emotions do have adaptive functions, you may not be successful*

in eliminating completely the negative emotion. Hence sublimate it (redirect it into a productive channel). For example, you may walk fast or do gardening when angry.

Negativity bias is a common human experience. It demonstrates a strong case that negative experience, or fear of bad events has a far greater effect on people than do neutral experiences or even positive experiences. The phenomenon may take the popular expression: *Bad is stronger than good* (or alternatively, the villain is better remembered than the hero).

A simple example can illustrate the concept. Suppose you are asked to form opinion about a person whose description reads: He is punctual and hardworking. He does his office work meticulously. He is also helpful to others. He keeps contact with others but he takes leave at the time of need.

What impression do you form of him? Is your overall impression positive or negative? It is found that most of the people form negative impression of this person. A single negative description neutralizes the positive impact produced by favourable trait-description and shifts people's overall impression towards the negative end.

The phenomenon is manifest in several domains of life. Parents should understand negativity bias because it can influence and shape parenting. Every day parents may provide children with many positive and neutral experiences. However, the day father or mother spanks the child is the day the child remembers. Similarly you are likely to remember the insult you received during your school days, even though you have also received compliment a number of times. Negative occurrences tend to resonate and be more memorable than positive or neutral experiences.

The concept of negativity bias explains as to why

candidates in an election use negative campaigning. Instead of propagating their achievements and positive projections, they paint the opposite candidate as someone to be feared. People may vote based not so much on the admiration of a particular candidate, but vote for the candidate who is unlikely to bring bad things (e.g., more taxes) into their lives.

The impact of negativity bias is reflected in the context of decision making. It has been found that recruiters are more eager to reject a candidate on the basis of negative trait than are eager to select someone on the basis of positive traits. The tendency to reject is more pronounced than the tendency to select in hiring decision.

The clearer demonstration of negativity bias in several domains of life raises fundamental questions of its causality. However, there is no single explanation; explanations are offered from various perspectives.

Evolutionary Perspective. The tendency to put more weight on negative entities than positive ones likely evolved for an important reason: to keep us out of harm's way. From the beginning of humanity it has been our most important survival skill to be able to stay away from danger. Knowing this survival technique, our brain has developed systems that make it hard for us to not notice danger and respond to it.

In the brain, there are two different systems for negative and positive stimuli. The left hemisphere, which is known for articulate language, is somewhat specialized for positive experience; whereas as right hemisphere focuses more on negative experiences. Another area of the brain used for the negative bias is the *amygdala*. This specific area of the brain uses about two-thirds of its neurons searching for experience. Once the amygdala starts looking for the bad news, it is stored into long-term memory. Positive experiences have to be held in awareness for more than twelve seconds in order for the transfer from short-term memory to long-term memory to take place. Cliff Nass, professor of communication from Stanford University has suggested managers offer praise *after* criticism, not before, so that the praise actually makes an impression on the receiver.

Emotion information revolves within the limbic system. Therefore, the limbic system ties perfectly into two negative bias. It may be indicated that limbic system (located in the brain-stem) was formed prior to the cortex, the thinking brain. It implies that the mechanism to deal with survival needs was given first. The neocortex – responsiblefor maintaining higher level cognitive processes – evolvedlater. A person uses the neocortex when trying to control the negative symptoms dispersed from the limbic system. Based on the connection between the limbic system and the nervous system, the body reacts harshly when solely speaking about negative events.

Factors of Novelty and Distinctiveness. In view of the fact that negative information is non-normal, it is more distinctive and more novel compared to positive information. The fact that it has more novelty means it will be remembered and more easily recalled. The fact that it is distinctive means that it is distinguishable among different objects. If the negative message eliminates its surprised factor, it will reduce the impact of the negative information.

Generally negative information is considered more informative. For example, interviewees in a job interview behave in a polite and agreeable manner. If a candidate behaves aggressively and rudely, it gives out much information about the candidate's traits. Thus the behaviour is more informative and more credible than normative positive information.

In conclusion, it is important to recognize that negativity bias is a fact of individual and collective life. Yet, the correct explanation of the bias requires more systematic and controlled studies in future.

2. THE PRINCIPLE OF Positivity Ratios:

People with higher positivity ratios (proportion of positive emotion to negative emotion) have superior mental health and adjustment than those with lower ratios. Gottman's work famously shows that successful close relations are characterized by positivity ratios of about 5:1.

THE APPLICATION:

*Follow the technique of **capitalization**. The basic idea here is that positive emotions have beneficial effects that are both independent of and beyond those of negative emotions. That is in addition to offsetting the ill-effects of negative affect, positive emotions independently enhance the quality of our lives.*

In current conceptualization of well-being, a distinction has been made between happiness and human flourishing. Human flourishing is beyond happiness in that it encompasses both feeling good and doing good. This definition is based on the fundamental work of Keyes (2002). It conceptualizes and measures human flourishing as a multidimensional combination of hedonic and eudaimonic well-being. Following ancient philosophies articulated by Aristotle, hedonic well-being captures individuals' global satisfaction with life alongside their pleasant affects, whereas eudiamonic well-being encompasses their sense of purpose and meaning as well as their resilience and social integration.

Fredrickson and Losada specify this "feel good plus do good" definition. To flourish means to live within an optional range of human functioning one that connotes goodness, generativity, growth, and resilience (Fredrickson & Losada, 2005). Thus the construct of flourishing includes both feeling good (i.e., hedonic) and functioning effectively (i.e., eudaimonia). In this way it is the mirror opposite of common mental disorder such as depression and anxiety, which encompasses negative (or flat) affect and poor functioning.

Feeling good, however, does more than simply reflect the presence of human flourishing. From the perspective of the broaden-and-build theory, positivity takes on a far more vital role with respect to human flourishing. Beyond being one dimension of flourishing, positive emotions have also been found to promote the development and maintenance of flourishing. It has been demonstrated that daily experiences of positive emotions forecast and produce growth in personal resources such as competence, meaning, optimism, resilience, self-acceptance, positive relationship, and physical health. In other words, feeling good does not simply sit side by side with optimal functioning as an indicator of flourishing. Feeling good drives optimal functioning by building resources upon which people draw to navigate life's journey with greater success.

Since flourishing is associated with a greater number of positive effects, a fundamental question concerns positivity ratio: How many positive effects would neutralize the effect of a single negative affect? Fredrickson and Losada (2005) suggest that flourishing is associated with higher positivity ratios than nonflourishing. They maintain that the mean positivity ratio for flourishers is

3.2:1, whereas for nonflourishers it is 2.3:1. In other words, the person should have three good days for every single bad day. Put differently, a single day in which negative emotion prevails has the countervailing force of three good days.

It is suggested that "a good first estimate" for the affect balance necessary for minimal emotional well-being would be value of pi (π or 3.14).

The most extensive studies of positivity ratios were conducted by John Gottman and his colleagues (1999). Among his many studies were intensive observations of married couples in his "Love-lab". This was an apartment set up to videotape verbal, nonverbal, and physiological responses of couples as they talked about topics of conflict and how they viewed each other's strength and weaknesses. The main objective was to get couples talk and to analyze their style of communication. Both the husbands' and wives' verbal and nonverbal behaviours were carefully recorded. Observations captured both subtle nonverbal behaviours (like a faint frown or raised eyebrows), and more obvious behaviours (such as smiling, one spouse interrupting the other and expression of anger, resentment, affection, and support).

Gottman's work famously shows that successful marriages are characterized by positivity ratio of about 5:1, whereas marriages on cascades towards dissolution have ratios of about 1:1. The basic message sent out by this finding posits the principle of **capitalization**: neutralize negativity by more and more positivity.

3. THE PRINCIPLE OF Transelection :

Higher is better, within bounds

THE APPLICATION:
Since there is no such thing as an unmitigated good, increase levels of positive emotions up to a point.

While principle of *capitalization* suggests more and more positives for neutralizing adverse effect of negative effects and for promoting flourishing mental health, there is a limit. Evidence has mounted to support the ancient wisdom that people can get 'too much of a good thing", experiencing a downturn in good outcomes with disproportional levels of positive emotion (Fredrickson, 2013).

Research on how positive emotions go awry in the context of bipolar disorder is illustrative here. Bipolar disorder, also known as manic-depressive illness, is one of the top 10 causes of disability worldwide and has long been characterized by abnormally elevated positive mood during manic episodes.

Within the spectrum of normative emotional experience, the notion that excessive positivity might be harmful is consistent with the long standing evidence that life satisfaction is better predicted by **the frequency rather than the intensity** of a person's positive emotions. The most frequently experienced positive emotions are the mild and moderate ones. Whereas increasing levels of positive emotions bring benefits up to a point, extremely high levels of emotions carry costs that begin to outweigh these benefits. This classic, nonmonotonic U-shaped relationship has been found between positive emotions and a range of desired outcomes (e.g., emotional stability, creativity, longevity).

Drawing on these observations, some researches make the case for 'a fundamental psychological principle: There is no such thing as an unmitigated good". They argue that research programmes now need to focus on identifying the presence and specific location of *inflection points*. Although Fredrickson and Losada (2005) have suggested a tipping point, at positivity ratios of about 11:1, more studies are needed to draw definitive conclusion. The safest conclusion to draw is that an inverted-U inflection point exists and **"higher is better, within bounds"**.

4. **THE PRINCIPLE OF**
Resource:
Positive emotions broaden the scope of vital engagement and build internal resources
THE APPLICATION:
Cultivate positive emotions and do works that induce positive emotion (e.g., helping behaviour).

Our evolutionary heritage has given us the capacity to experience a rich array of emotions. We can feel sad, happy, anxious, surprised, bored and frustrated. We may feel the bittersweet combination of both sadness and joy. These emotions come in two basic forms, namely positive and negative affect. **Positive effects** include emotions such as joy, love, compassion and happiness. **Negative effects** include anger, fear, sadness and depression.

Positive and negative affects constitute a basic structure of people's emotional lives. The differences in levels of positive and negative emotional experiences are significantly related to well-being. Furthermore, physiological studies show a distinctive pattern of nervous system arousal, brain activity, hormonal, and neurotransmitter output that distinguishes positive from negative emotions. In other words, our bodies display something different when we are in a positive emotional state and when we are in a negative motional state.

However, it is hard to tell whether someone is happy or joyful.

As pointed out earlier, potential value of positive emotions has been stressed in many contexts. While adaptive significance for both negative and positive emotions has been recognized, the time scale is different. Negative emotions carried adaptive significance in the moment that our human ancestors experienced them. For example, the tendency to fight or flee drove behaviours that saved life. Positive emotions, by contrast, carried adaptive significance for our human ancestors over longer time scales. Having a broadened mindset is not a key ingredient in the recipe for any quick survival mechanism. However, it is a mechanism for discovery of new knowledge, new alliance and new skills.

Barbara Fredrickson's (2001) *broaden-and-build theory* of positive emotions provides an overview of how positive emotions help build physical, psychological and social resources. The theory describes how positive emotions open up our thinking and actions to new possibilities, and how these expansions can help build physical, psychological and social resources.

In the classical experimental demonstration, Fredrickson and her colleagues asked research participants to watch emotionally charged film clips. The clips were selected for the purpose of inducing one of four emotions: joy, contentment, anger or fear. A neutral, nonemotional clip served as a control condition. After watching the film clip, participants were asked to think of a situation that created feelings similar to those aroused by the film clip. Given the feelings created by the imagined situation, they were asked to list all the things they would like to do right then. The results of this study supported the broaden-and-build theory. People in the joy and contentment conditions described more things they would like to do right then, than people in the anger or fear conditions. Further, people experiencing anger or fear identified fewer describable actions than people in the neutral, nonemotional control condition. The broadening of thought-action possibilities, resulting from positive emotions helps build intellectual resources for solving important life problems, because the more options we consider, the more likely we are to find an effective solution.

Negative emotions tend to narrow our thoughts to a limited set of possible actions that might be taken in response to an emotion-evoking situation. When we are angry or fearful, we become self-focused and absorbed in the emotion. This may result in a kind of tunnel vision and an unduly limited consideration of all possibilities. It is hard to think in a free and creative way when we are angry or fearful. In contrast, positive emotions seem to open up people's thinking to a wider array of possible actions. Perhaps because we are not so self-focused, more options and ways of thinking about a situation come to mind when we are content or happy than when we are upset.

5. **THE PRINCIPLE OF Gender:**
> *Women indicate greater affective intensity than do men. Thus, women experience high levels of positive affect as well as negative affect.*

THE APPLICATION:
> *Women report as much global happiness as do men (with respect to affective intensity, the range is higher in women vis-à-vis men, yet the mean is approximately the same).*
> Women frequently report being just as happy as men.

The findings that women report being as happy as men and women report being depressed at twice the rate that men do seem contradictory. Some researchers argue that women are actually unhappy, but they report in surveys that they are happy because of a need to conform to social norms-one of which is being happy. This explanation, however, makes it difficult to account for women's self-reported higher negative affect. If women falsely report being happy only to appear being happy they would not accurately report experiencing high levels of negative affect.

In view of this complexity, Fugita, Diener and Sandvik (1991) proposed that gender differences in affect intensity can explain the paradoxical presence of both the greater prevalence of negative affect and the equal (or greater) overall happiness reported by women.

According to Fujita et.al. (1991), affect intensity is the individual difference variable that refers to one's response intensity to a given level of emotion-provoking situation. People who experience high levels of negative emotion intensity also tend to have very intense positive emotions. One of the costs is the experiencing of more intense negative emotions.

If people who experience high levels of positive affect also experience high levels of negative affect, it is possible that these people would report much more distress while also reporting equal levels of overall wellbeing. Fujita et.al. (1991) posit that women have greater emotional intensity than men. This allows them to experience both more joy and more sorrow. These gender differences in affective experience can be used as a basis for explaining the gender differences in depression. Moreover, the concept of affect intensity is equally proficient in explaining women's equal overall well-being.

6. THE PRINCIPLES OF
Culture and Display Rules:
>Six primary emotions (happiness, sadness, fear, anger, surprise, and disgust) have been identified. These emotions may produce a blend in the expression depending on the cultural context. Furthermore, expression of emotion is governed by culture-specific display rules.

THE APPLICATION:
>Learn and use cultural intelligence to identify and respond appropriately to others' emotion.

Darwin (1872) has stressed that emotions are crucial to human existence and the expression of emotion serve important functions of adaptation. Despite this early work that indicated universalism, psychologists have examined the cultural influence on emotional behaviours. Consequently two streams of research have surfaced, one dealing with the issue of *universality* and the other pertaining to *culture-specificity*.

Paul Ekman (1972) is a pioneering researcher in this area. He suggests that emotions are expressed in a universally similar manner. Of-course, studies have mostly been carried out on the facial expressions of emotion. It is assumed that the face is exposed to the full view of others for the facility of social interaction; the face provides a link between expressive behaviour and subjective reaction. Tomkin emphasized that the face is the primary locus of emotional behaviour.

An emotional expression is a consequence of an elicitor that triggers the innate facial affect programme, and is modulated by display rules. Ekman observed that the elicitor (for example, a social situation) may differ from culture to culture but the facial behaviour in response to it (for example, an angry response) conveys a similar meaning to the representatives of all cultures. By facial affect programme, Ekman meant the expression of primary emotions via a combination of facial muscular movements which are neutrally connected. Six primary emotions have been identified: *happiness, sadness, fear, anger, surprise, and disgust.*

These primary emotions may produce a blend in the expression depending on the cultural contexts. For example, sadness and surprise may produce an expression of disappointment. In addressing the universal aspect of emotion, Ekman accommodated the culture-bound issues by analyzing the concept of *display rules*. These are a set of socially-learned behaviours that may modify the facial appearance either by a voluntary decision or by the autonomic subconscious habits.

Several examples of display rules can be cited. *Amplification* refers to the act of expressing an emotion more intensely than what is truly felt. In Russian parliament, members of parliament are expected to display greater happiness and clap more loudly when a bill is passed. *Deamplification* is the opposite process. People are expected to express their emotion less intensely than what is truly felt. For example, Westerners are expected not to display their actual sadness when they are around a dead body. Similarly *neutralizing* denotes the act of displaying nothing and displaying some other emotion than what is truly felt. Finally, *qualification* refers to the act of displaying an emotion with another, blended simultaneously or occurring sequentially in time. The display rules are learned during the process of development and culture training. These are also influenced by personal (age, sex, and attitude) and situational (type of relationship) factors within a culture. It has been shown that the Japanese mask the feeling of anger with a smile. The British tend to deintensify the expressions of most emotions. Westerners, in general, inhibit negative emotions (sadness) in public and openly express happiness. Easterners, in contrast, tend to inhibit positive emotions and display negative emotion (sadness).

Based on such empirical evidence, Ekman (1982) put forward a neurocultural theory of emotion. He maintains that the expression of basic emotions are triggered by an innate facial affect programme and the culture-specific display rules modify these emotion expressions to suit the social relevance and context.

The *elements of culture-specificity* may be attributed to marked variation in the cultural display rules. The various factors contributing to such variations include cultural differences in individualism/collectivism, power distance, and ingroup/outgroup mindset. For example, the negative emotion such as fear and anger are rarely expressed with full intensity because these practices are often considered as a defiance of social norms in collective societies (Mandal, 2004).

Izard is another prominent researcher in the area of human emotion. He examined the cross-cultural differences in response to his emotion attitude questionnaire: Which emotion do you understand the best? Which emotion do you dread the most? Which negative emotion do you experience most frequently? Izard found cultural differences. While most cultural groups indicated joy/enjoyment as the best understood emotion, the British and the French indicated interest/excitement as the best understood and most preferred category. The Japanese considered disgust/ contempt as the most dreaded emotion, other cultures opted for the fear/ terror category as the dreaded one. For the item which negative emotion is experienced most frequently experienced, sex-specificity was observed across the cultures, the males in every culture selected the disgust/contempt category.

7. THE PRINCIPLE OF Facial Asymmetry:

The socially learned display rules are more prominent in the right side of the face than the left side of the face.

THE APPLICATION :

Learn that two sides of the face are not equally expressive.

It is important to consider the interaction between cultural factors and neuropsychological elements. For example, neuropsychological research has shown that the two sides of the human face are not equally expressive. The right side of the face (controlled by the left hemisphere that mediates cognitive behaviour) offers socially appropriate clues whereas its left side (controlled by the right hemisphere that mediates emotional process) divulges hidden personal feelings. The socially learned display rules are more prominent in the right side of the face (as this side exhibits culturally varied expressions) than the left side of the face (as this side is more or less invariant to race or culture). This difference suggests that cross-cultural neuropsychology in emotion communication is an emerging area of interest.

Putting It All Together

There is nothing obscure about these seven principles of human emotion. They neatly codify our understanding of the ways people experience and express emotions. These principles are easy for most people to grasp. However, I have learned to stress two major points.

First, although the seven principles and their applications have been discussed in the context of human flourishing, their importance for the management of self and others is highly pertinent. While applying, they should be applied in combination to compound their impact. For example, the principle of positivity ratios directs us to build relationship on the basis of capitalization (sending out more and more positive emotional signals), but principle of transelection offers appropriate guidelines for respecting a limit.

Second, although emotions are stronger than thoughts (cognitions), it would not be judicious to make watertight compartmentalization between affect and cognitions. While understanding and regulating emotions, an adequate grasp of certain basic principles of cognitive functioning is essential. People skilled in both the domains (cognitions and emotions) are likely to secure achievements of commendable magnitude.

Chapter 14

Savouring

Modern life is too hectic. We walk fast, talk fast and eat our food very fast. The fast food restaurants are mushrooming even in developing countries. Although the fastness in our activities is not all that bad, the situation of missing good moments in life is disturbing. Savouring, in this context, is offered as a model of utilizing good moments in life and increasing the intensity and frequency of our positive experiences.

The basic assumption of **savouring** is that *people have capacities to attend to, appreciate and enhance the positive experiences in their lives.* Savouring may occur spontaneously, we may find ourselves captivated by a striking sunset, or by surging clouds, or by fascinating waves, or by stretching mountains. Appreciation and enjoyment arise from immersing ourselves in beauties and bounties of nature.

We may also plan savouring. Whether planed or spontaneous, savouring requires some precondition. First, we must have a sense of immediacy of what is happening in the moment – here and now. This is a focused attention. It is easier to think in terms of objects or situations. A person may savour a sunset or a waterfall. A person may also savour an ongoing get-together.

However, it is possible to savour internal thoughts and feelings. A person may savour happy memories relating to childhood experiences. An individual may savour the anticipation of a future positive event such as marriage or graduation. In a group context, people's attention may be down towards a positive event and people may be encouraged to have rumination of positive memories. Of course, full absorption is needed for savouring to occur.

Second, the experience of savouring requires that certain other needs to set aside. For example, savouring does not occur if people are thinking about how others are viewing them. Similarly, extraneous thoughts relating to domestic responsibilities, children's studies, career-related thoughts and other intrusive thoughts spoil savouring. People have to intentionally ignore distracting matters; they have to settle for relaxation and disengagement. Savouring requires an attentive, but a quiet and relaxed state of mind.

Finally, savouring requires a mindful focus on the pleasurable aspect of a current experience. The person has to appreciate one particular thing rather than thinking of several things. We need take a break from analytical thinking and allow ourselves to get lost in a single thing.

Savouring is a self-aware activity. Thinking occurs, but it is focused on enhancing the experience. This is a process of attending to, thinking about, and identifying the emotions associated with savouring. The person can ask: 'what emotions am I experiencing?' Is the savouring emotion a feeling of warmth, comfort, joy, inspiration, happiness, pleasure, gratefulness, contentment, or connectedness? By focusing on the specifics, we may become more aware of the rich complexity of our emotions.

Savouring is a simple way to enhance our experiences. It is extremely useful to punctuate each day with savouring moments that unplug for a time from our hectic lives. With practice over time, savouring may become a general mindset applied to more and more aspects of life.

Chapter 15

Empathy

The growth of the concept of emotional intelligence (EI) is a major break-through in the Twenty-first Century. The analysis of its components reveals two interrelated domains of *intrapersonal* and *interpersonal* sensitivities of which empathy is the core concept. Prior to the systematic examination of mechanism of empathy, certain world events drew people's attention to the importance of empathy.

It is a common sense knowledge that Hitler's Nazi atrocities constitute a black chapter in human history. Six million Jews were butchered. The horrors of gas chambers and concentration camps created a fear psychosis. After the fall of Hitler, Jews rallied together to probe into some of the key questions: Why was there anti-semitism? How did Hitler manipulate press and people? Who are the main culprits and associates of Hitler who should be brought to justice?

In addition to these key questions, there was a positive question that received research attention from the Jewish Group. The Jewish Community was prettry aware that quite a number of Germans were sympathetic to the suffering of Jewish people. Some of them provided shelter and food to fleecing Jewish persons despite the risk of their lives. There was continuous and rigid search operations by Nazi Generals. Yet some Germans rendered valuable human service by protecting the Jewish at their own homes.

After the end of World War II, the Jewish Group undertook the project of identifying these benevolent Germans. In the meantime, many of them have grown old and some of them have passed away. The Jewish Research Team spotted their children who are now adults. The researchers had a strong assumption. They believed that these adult Germans who are now settled at different jobs at different places must have seen the scenarios of their parents' deeds. They must have seen with what courage and sacrifice their parents have had protected the Jewish people.

The researchers were interested to examine the impact of such early experience. They found that it had tremendous impact. Not only their parents were benevolent, they themselves are also benevolent. They are eager to help others; their life-style is oriented towards prosocial behaviour.

This observation clearly illustrates that a compassionate life is possible despite the age-old cynicism that people are utterly selfish. Of-course, a more systematic and scientific research commenced in the last part of the Twentieth Century. It heralded the grandeur and beauty of emotional intelligence encompassing empathy.

The entry of the construct of emotional intelligence represents a *paradigm shift* in behavioural science. The twentieth century, for its most part, was a century of rational intelligence. The construct of rational intelligence and its operational counterpart IQ was introduced in 1904. It was in response to the request of French Education Ministry in Paris. The Ministry people sought help from psychologists to devise some mechanism so that children could be classified into three categories: the average, achieving, and underachieving. It was thought that such a classification of students into three categories would equip teachers to adopt three different styles appropriate for their acquisition.

Fortunately a French psychologist Binet was successful in devising a method. Measurement of rational intelligence (main component: reasoning) developed in a big way. The movement spread to other parts of Europe, America and the entire Globe. Rational intelligence was expressed in terms of Intelligence Quotients (IQ^s).

While the concept of intelligence surfaced as an attempt to quantify the capacity for learning, it was found to be a strong and stable predictor of school and college achievement. Objectively rational intelligence accounted for almost fifty percent of variance in academic achievement. It was also a good predictor of job success.

Because of the very high predictive role of rational intelligence, it dominated the intellectual climate almost for a century. Then caveats began to appear. Several threats were posed. A number of critics pointed out the very low, though positive, correlation between creativity and intelligence. This implies that a person with moderate intelligence can be highly creativity. Others highlighted the concept of multiple intelligence (such as mathetical intelligence, musical intelligence, environmental intelligence, etc) in place of unitary general intelligence.

However, the heaviest blow came from the works of neuroscientists. During the second half of the Twentieth Century, there were tremendous growths in the study of brain functions. The new and innovative techniques of MRI, fMRI and PET provided on accurate picture of brain functions. Neuroscientific findings showed that our thinking brain (seat of IQ) is not as old as our feeling brain.

When organisms were evolving and they were at a reptile stage, some ring-like structures began to form near brain-stem (where the spiral cord is ending and brain is starting). Since *limbus* is the Greek word for ring, experts called it limbic system. The *limbic system* took care of our emotion. Although brain is structurally one, functionally it has two parts: feeling brain and thinking brain. Feeling brain is older than the thinking brain. Perhaps Nature gave us first what was needed first.

Subsequently it was also discovered that brain has lateralization. A thick neural fibre divides the brain into two halves: the left hemisphere and right hemisphere. The left hemisphere takes care of language and logic; right hemisphere takes care of pattern and emotion. Interestingly the left hemisphere is connected with right limbs neutrally and the vice versa. This implies that left ear is more adaptive to listening music. The sound stimuli would pass through left ear and would be transmitted to right hemisphere which is specialized in processing patterns of sound.

Viewed from this perspective, left hemisphere is the seat for IQ whereas right hemisphere is seat for EQ (Emotional Quotient). Now behavioural scientists argue that IQ contributes only 20 percent of our lifetime success whereas the rest comes from emotional intelligence. Since emotional intelligence has been neglected in the past, the present-day scientists call upon to rectify this lopsided development.

Emotional Intelligence has these main components:
1. Self-Awareness
2. Self-skill (tolerance, self-control)
3. Social awareness (Interpersonal sensitivity)
4. Social skill

5. Self-Motivation
6. Optimism and positive mood

In summary, empathy as a seminal concept within the framework of emotional intelligence receives greater recognition. Empathy refers to the ability of taking others' perspective and experiencing others' feelings.

Dynamics of Empathy

Empathy typically has both emotional and cognitive components, although these components can be experienced separately. Emotional empathy is the vicarious experiencing of another's emotional state, which children may experience in some form as early as infancy and toddlerhood. In contrast, cognitive empathy, which is also sometimes referred to as *theory of mind* or *perspective taking*, is the ability to accurately imagine another's experience. As children enter the preschool and elementary school years, there are significant gains particularly in the area of cognitive empathy. This is particularly because the children's increased language capacities facilitate empathetic reflections.

By preschool age (4-5 years), children are generally capable of taking another's perspective in false belief tasks, which is a frequently used indicator of theory of mind development. During false belief tasks, children are typically presented with a scenario with two characters, during which one of the characters place an item in a given location and leaves the room. Then, the second character arrives and move the item to a new place. When the first character re-enters the room, the participating child is asked where the first character will look for the item. If the child has a theory of mind, she should respond with the original location rather than the true location. This would indicate a capability to see the situation from the perspective of the character who left the room. The ability to understand others' perspectives is integral for fully and successfully identifying with another's experience.

While these two aspects of empathy typically occur together once they are developed, they can also develop unequally. A couple of examples may illustrate the occurrence in adults. Suppose a patient is describing his plight to a doctor. If empathetic, the door would first mentally lower down to the level of a patient. He would take patient's perspective and imagine patient's plain. Then the doctor would experience emotional empathy. He would feel sad to share with patient's sadness.

Similarly an employee may report his achievements to his employer. If empathetic, the employer would adopt employee's perspective and would place himself mentally at the position of an employee. Then there would be emotional sharing. Because the employee is happy, the employer would experience happiness. This is emotional empathy.

It has been indicated that cognitive and emotional empathy may occur together; they can also occur independently. Such a possibility exists because separate brain centres are involved for cognitive and emotional empathy.

There are several areas of the brain implicated in empathy. There is evidence that a special class of motor neurons, referred to as *mirror neurons,* respond similarly to the perception of action in others. These neurons lie in premotor and surrounding areas of the frontal and parietal lobes.

According to experts, viewing another's emotional state automatically and unconsciously activate one's personal associations with that state, causing, in the absence of inhibition one to react to another's experience as one would to one's own. The mirror neuron system may explain how this automatic state matching occurs in the brain.

In order to induce empathy, mirror neurons must communicate with other areas of the brain. The insular cortex has been shown to connect premotor mirror neurons to the limbic system, which processes the emotional aspect of empathy inducing situations. The limbic system is an evolutionarily older area of the brain involved in the experiencing of emotions. Different areas of the limbic system may process different types of emotional stimuli associated with empathy. For example, the anterior insula and anterior cingulated cortex are activated when viewing disgust expressions while the amygdala is activated when observing faces displaying fear or distress.

In order to experience empathy and not become overwhelmed with personal distress, neural mechanisms involved in emotion regulation must be activated. The prefrontal cortex appears to be important for the reducing the personal distress. This allows the observer to connect on a more cognitive level with the other's experience and aides in helping behaviour.

Contributors to Empathy Development

The ability to empathize typically develops early and rapidly. Several factors facilitate the development of empathy in the young children. Contributions such as genetics, neural development, temperaments and socialization.

Genetic Factors. In a longitudinal study of twins, both genetic and environmental components were implicated in the development of empathy. In this study, young children's responses to simulated distress were measured in monozygotic ("identical") and dizygotic ("fraternal") twins at 14 and 20 months of age. The premise of this study design is not the degree to which the correlation in empathy levels is greater among monozygotic than dizygotic twins reflects the impact of heredity.

Neurodevelopmental Factors. There are several areas of the brain implicated in empathetic behaviour and empathy development. Studies of monkeys have revealed a special class of motor neurons, referred to as *mirror neurons,* that respond similarly to the perception of actions in others and the production of in oneself. There is evidence that the human brain contains a *similar mirror neuron system,* which lies in premotor and surrounding areas of the frontal and parietal lobes. On their own, mirror neurons and the mirror neuron system are not responsible for empathetic feelings, they are thought to provide a neural basis for connecting our own and others experiences.

According to the theorist de Waal, viewing another's emotional state automatically and unconsciously activate one's personal associations with that state, causing one to react to another's experience as one would to one's own. This automatic state matching is thought to form the basis for higher levels of empathy.

In order to induce empathy mirror neurons must communicate with many other areas of the brain. The insular cortex has been shown to connect premotor neurons to the limbic system which process the emotional aspect of empathy inducing situations. The limbic system is an evationarily older arc of the brain involved in the experiencing of emotions. Different areas of the limbic system may process different types of emotional stimuli associated with empathy. For example the anterior insula and anterior cingulated cortex are activated when viewing disgust expressions, while the amygdala is activated when viewing fear or distress.

In order to experience empathy and not become overwhelmed with personal distress, neural mechanisms involved in emotion regulation must be activated. The prefrontal cortex appears to be important for reducing the personal distress that is activated in response to another's stress. This allows the observer to connect on a more cognitive level with the other's experience and aids in helping behaviour.

Parenting. Since parents and caregivers have a significant socializing influence on infants it follows that parenting would influence the early development of empathy. One aspect of parent-child interaction is the level of *synchrony* between parent and child. Synchronity is the matching of behaviour between relationship partners. Mother-child synchrony is directly associated with empathy levels in children. Specifically, the more mothers and infants matched and influenced each other's' behaviours during face-to-face play in infancy, the more empathy was expressed by the child during mother-child conversation.

In general, maternal warmth has been found to be an important factor in promoting empathy development. The way parents talk to their children about emotions also appears to affect empathy development. The degree to which parents direct their children label emotions is associated with children's emotional concern for others. The degree to which parents provide explanations concerning the causes and consequences of emotions is associated with more attempts by the child to understand others' emotion. Taken together, it seems that parents who provide a warm, positive environment for their children, and who provide a model for being sensitive to others' needs and emotion are most likely to have empathetic children.

Chapter 16

Attitude of Gratitude

It is a truism that how you think --- about yourself, your world, and other people --- is more important to your well-being than the objective circumstances of your life. "The mind is its own place, and in itself Can make a Heaven of Hell, a Hell of Heaven", John Milton wrote in *Paradise Lost*. Philosophers, writers, and great grand-mothers of times past have long highlighted the benefits of positive thinking. While there are several ways to boost positive thinking, the expression of gratitude is an effective strategy for achieving well-being.

Gratitude is many things to many people. It is wonder; it is appreciation; it is looking at the brighter side of a setback; it is fathoming abundance; it is thanking someone in your life; it is thanking God; it is **"counting blessings"**. The average person, however, probably associates gratitude with saying thank you for a gift or benefit received.

The world's most prominent researcher and writer about gratitude, Robert Emmons, defines it as "a felt sense of wonder, thankfulness, and appreciation for life". You feel grateful by noticing how fortunate your circumstances are. By definition, the practice of gratitude involves a focus on present moment, on appreciating your life as it is today and what has made it so.

Expressing gratitude is a lot more than saying thank you. Emerging research has recently shown multiple benefits. People who are consistently grateful have been found to be relatively happier, more energetic, and more hopeful. They report experiencing more frequent positive emotions. They also tend to be more helpful and empathetic, more spiritual and religious, more forgiving and less materialistic than others who are less predisposed to gratefulness. Furthermore, the more a person is inclined to gratitude, the less likely he or she is to be depressed, anxious, lonely, envious and neurotic. All these research findings are correlational; we cannot know whether being grateful causes all these good benefits or possessing good things make people grateful.

In the very first set of studies, one group of participants was asked to write down five things for which they were thankful --- namely, to count their blessings --- and to do so once a week for ten weeks in a row. Other groups of participants were asked to think about other five daily hassles or five major events that occurred to them. The findings were exciting. Relative to the control group, those participants counting their blessings tended to feel more optimistic and more satisfied with their lives. Even their health received a boost; they reported fewer physical symptoms.

In another study the effect of strategy of counting one's blessing was investigated. Participants were asked to keep a sort of gratitude journal – to write down and contemplate five things for which they felt grateful. The exact instructions were as follows: "There are many things in our lives, both large and small, that we might be grateful about. Think back over the events of the past week and write down on the lines below up to five things that happened for which you are grateful or thankful". Five lines followed, headed by "This week I am grateful for".

The participants were engaged in this intervention over the course of six weeks. Half of the participants were instructed to do it once a week (every Sunday night), and half to do it three times a week (every Tuesday, Thursday, and Sunday). As expected, participants involved in intervention showed greater happiness than control group participants.

There are several explanations for positive effects of counting blessings. First, grateful thinking promotes the memory and positive life experiences. By taking pleasure in some of the gifts of your life, you will be able to extract the maximum possible satisfaction and enjoyment from your current circumstances. Second, expressing gratitude bolsters self-worth and self-esteem. When you realize how much people have done for you or how much you have accomplished, you feel more confident and efficacious. Third, gratitude helps people cope with stress. Expressing gratefulness during personal adversity can help you adjust, move on and perhaps begin anew. Fourth, the expression of gratitude encourages moral behaviours. Fifth, gratitude can help build social bonds, strengthening existing relationship and nurturing new ones. Sixth, expressing gratitude tends to inhibit insidious comparisons with others. Seventh, the practice of gratitude is incompatible with negative emotions and may actually diminish or deter such feeling as anger, bitterness and greed.

Practice of Gratitude
It is advisable to practice gratitude. There are several ways. People can choose a strategy that fits with their personality and attitude.

Gratitude journal. If you enjoy writing, choose a time of day when you have several minutes to step outside your life and reflect. It may be the first thing in the morning, or during lunch, or before bedtime. Ponder the three to five things for which you are currently grateful. The events may range from the mundane (your TV set is fixed, your flowers are finally in bloom, your spouse got you a gift) to the magnificent experiences (your children received awards).

Paths to gratitude. Some of you may not enjoy writing. You may contemplate. Choose one thing each day. You may think of a particular goal and try to recollect the help and assistance you have received in the context of this goal fulfillment. This strategy would help to count your blessings in an effective manner.

Keep the strategy fresh. If you have been practicing a strategy for a long time (say, writing the events), you may become bored with the routine and may cease to extract much meaning from it. You should now change the strategy. Talk to a friend, express gratitude through art (photography, wall magazines) you may purposefully vary the mode of communicating the gratitude messages.

Direct expression. Express gratitude directly to another. The use of phones, letters, emails and face-to-face communication are recommended. Express your appreciation in concrete terms. The target persons may be your parents, favorite uncle, or old friend, old coach, teacher or supervisor. Write him or her a letter now. If possible, visit and read the letter out loud in person, on either a special day (birthday, anniversary). Describe in detail what he or she has done for you and how it has influenced your life. Some people find it uplifting to write gratitude letters to individuals whom they don't know personally.

Have you ever written letters of gratitude to your

teachers / professors who have impacted your life in a significant way? Have you written letters of thankfulness to writers / poets who have made an impact on your taste and temperaments? Have you expressed gratitude to artists whose contributions you adore? *If you have not done it in the past, do it now.*

There are multiple ways to practice the strategy of gratitude, it would be wise to choose what works best for you. *Select at least one option and give it a go.* When the strategy loses its freshness or meaningfulness, don't hesitate to make a change in how, when, and how often you express yourself.

Chapter 17

Building Flourishing Relationship

The capacity for love is a central component of all human societies. Love in all its manifestations, whether for children, parents, friends, or romantic partners, gives depth to human relationships. Specifically, love brings people close to each other physically and emotionally. When experienced intensely, it makes people feel expansively about themselves and the world.

While love has been depicted in classical literature in the past, contemporary behavioural scientists have attempted to identify its various components at an empirical level. Love for a companion is considered central to life well lived. Romantic love may not be essential in life, but it may be essential for joy. Life without love would be for many people like a black-and-white movie full of events and activities but without the colour that gives vibrancy and provides a sense of celebration.

A step-wise conceptualization of romantic love may foster an understanding of how it develops between two people.

Stage 1: Passionate and Companionate Aspects.
Romantic love is a complex emotion that may be best parsed into *passionate* and *companionate* forms. Passionate

love (the intense arousal that fuels a romantic union) involves a state of absorption between two people that often is accompanied by moods ranging from ecstasy to anguish. Companionate love (the soothing, steady warmth that sustains a relationship) is manifested on a strong bond and intertwining of lives that bring about feelings of comfort and peace. These two forms can occur simultaneously or intermittently rather than sequentially.

Romantic love is characterized by intense arousal and warm affection. During these stage partners seek knowledge about each other, they also use this knowledge to further their relationship. In a study of college students who were probably in the early stages of romantic relationship, nearly half named their romantic partners when asked to identify their closest friend. This suggests that passionate and companionate love can coexist in the new relationships of young people. Likewise, in a study of couples married for as long as 40 years, researchers found that companionate love and passionate love were alive, and that passionate love was the strongest predictor of marital satisfaction.

Stage 2: The Triangular Components of Love.

In developing a triangular theory of love, psychologist Robert Sternberg opine that love is a mix of three components: (1) passion, or physical attractiveness and romantic drives, (2) intimacy, or feeling of closeness and connectedness, and (3) commitment, involving the decision to initiate and sustain a relationship. Various combinations of these three components held eight forms of love. For example, intimacy and passion combined produce romantic love, whereas intimacy and commitment together constitute companionate love. Consummate love, the most durable type, is manifested when all three components (passion, intimacy and commitment) are present at high levels and in balance across both partners.

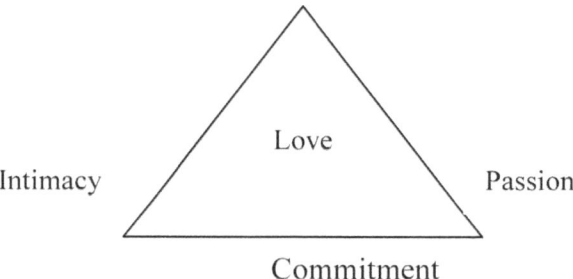

Consummate (Couple) Love = Intimacy + Commitment + Passion
Romantic Love = Intimacy + Passion
Friendship = Intimacy + Commitment
Infatuation = Passion only
Empty Love = Commitment only (Commercial Relation)
Fatuous Love = Passion + Commitment

Intimacy refers to mutual understanding, warm affection and mutual concern for the other's welfare. **Passion** means strong emotion, excitement, and physical arousal, often tied to sexual desire and attraction. **Commitment** is the conscious decision to stay in a relationship for a long period. It includes a series of devotion to the relationship and a willingness, to work on maintaining it. By putting together different combinations of the three ingredients, Sternberg's model describes several varieties of love and the specific components of romantic and companionate love.

High intimacy and passion describes romantic love in Sternberg's model. It may seem strange not to include commitment, but Sternberg argues that commitment is not a defining feature of romantic love. A winter romance, for example, may involve intimate mutual disclosure and strong passion, but no commitment to continue the relationship at winter's end.

Companionate love is a slow-developing love built on high intimacy and strong commitment. When youthful passion fades in a marriage, companionate love, based on deep, affectionate friendship provides a solid foundation for a lasting and successful relationship.

Both **fatuous love** (passion + commitment) and **infatuated love** (passion only) types might be regarded as forms of immature, blind or unreasonable love built on passion. Fatuous love combines high passion and commitment with an absence of intimacy. This would describe people who hardly know each other, but are caught up in a whirlwind passionate romance. Their commitment is based on passion and sustained solely by passion. Because passion is likely to fade with time, fatuous love relationships are unlikely to last. The same can be said for infatuated love, based only on passion, without intimacy or commitment. This might describe a teen romance in which sexual passion is taken for love. Infatuated love may also describe the sense of awe, adoration, and sex-related feelings that some people have for their favorite. Bollywood movie or music celebrity.

Empty Love (commitment only) includes no passion, no intimacy, just a commitment to stay together. Appropriately called empty love, this would describe an emotionally "dead" relationship that both members find some reason to continue. Reasons might include things such as convenience financial benefits, a sense of obligation or duty.

Consummate or complete love (intimacy + passion + commitment) is marked by high intimacy, passion and commitment. It is a form of love that many people desire. As in romantic love, the passionate component typically decreases over time. Yet, other components remain strong and grow. Sternberg's three-component model of love has received good empirical support. People's understanding of love's primary features and the differences among various types of relationships appear to fit well with the intimacy / passion / commitment conception. It is obvious to surmise that these components grow as love becomes more and more mature and sustainable.

Stage 3: The Self-Expansion of Romantic Love

Humans have a basic motivation to expand the self; the emotions, cognitions and behaviours of love fuel such self-expansion. People seek to expand themselves through love.

According to self-expansion theory, relationship satisfaction is a natural by-product of self-expressive love. Being in a loving relationship makes people feel good. They then associate these positive feelings with the relationship, thereby reinforcing their commitment to relationship. The positive consequences of being in love are clear. Researchers find that those who fall in love experience increased self-esteem and self-efficacy. On a more cognitive level, self-expansion means that each partner has made a decision to include another in his or her self. This investment in each other adds to relationship satisfaction. Each of the partners makes a greater use of the expression "we" instead of "I". This inclusivity is a prominent feature of flourishing relationship.

Another relationship involves a culture of appreciation. Generally, it is a human weakness that we tend to explain our success in terms of internal (dispositional) factors and explain failure in terms of external (environmental) factors. For example, we consider ourselves as bright if we complete a work successfully. In contrast, we blame the situational (environmental) difficulty if we fail. But we do not use similar yard sticks to explain others' success / failure. If others succeed, we give credit to situational parameters. If others fail, we blame their dispositional (personality) inadequacy.

What about the explanatory style in the context of flourishing relationship? If a wife fails in fixing the dinner in time, how does the husband explain the event? Is it because of the carelessness of wife or because of some unexpected arrival of guests in home? Needless to say as relationship flourishes, each of the partners takes an adaptive explanatory style. For success, he/she appreciates the other's positive disposition. For failure, he/she looks at the environmental constraints. This kind of explanatory style is a mark of maturing relationship.

The research on love also describes the meaning of "I love you". In a number of studies, the meaning of the statement, "I love you" has been analyzed. When participants are asked to describe exactly what they meant when they say "I love you" a variety of answers are generated. Some of the answers include: I understand; I support you, I am thankful to you. Ours is a good life; It is good to be with you. The variability in the meaning of these expressions suggests the complexity and richness of the emotion of love.

Well-minded relationships are healthy and long

lasting. The following exhibit depicts the sequence in flourishing relationship.

Adaptive	Nonadaptive
• An in-depth knowing process both partners seek to know and to be known by the other	No special effort to know or to be known by other
• Both partners use the knowledge gained in enhancing relationship	Knowledge gained is not used
• Both partners accept what they learn and respect the other for the person they learn about	Acceptance of what is learned is low
• Both partners in time develop a sense of being special and appreciated in the relationship	One or both partners fail to develop a sense of being special and appreciated in the relationship

Chapter 18

Spirituality

Spirituality as a topic in psychology has received mixed receptions. A number of psychologists in the 20th century ignored it; some psychologists viewed this as a topic in philosophy while others equated it with psychopathology. Despite such neglect, spirituality can't be dismissed as a "cultural fact". A vast majority of people believe in God and believe that God can be reached through prayer. People also believe that religion is important or very important in their lives. The importance of spirituality is perceived in a number of domains of human functioning such as mental health use of drug and alcohol, parenting, marital functioning and morality.

Defining Spirituality

Although many people describe themselves as spiritual, they define the term in many different ways. Definitions of spirituality have ranged from the best of that which is human to a quest for existential meaning, to the transcendent human dimension.

Traditionally many people equate spirituality with religious behaviour. However, contemporary writes contrast the two, suggesting that religion is dogmatic, institutional, and restrictive, whereas spirituality is personal, subjective and life-enhancing. Spirituality represents the key and unique function of religion. Spirituality is defined as **"a search for the sacred"**.

There are two key terms in this definition: search and the sacred. The term search indicates that spirituality is a process, one that involves efforts to discover the sacred and one that involves efforts to hold onto the sacred once it has been found. People can take a virtually limitless number of pathways in their attempts to discover and conserve the sacred. Spiritual pathways include social involvements that range from traditional religious institutions to non-traditional spiritual groups, programs and associations (e.g. Twelve Step meditation centers, Scientology). Pathways involve systems of belief that include those of traditional organized religions (Hindu, etc), newer spirituality movements (e.g. feminist, godless, ecological spiritualities), and more individualized world views.

In the *Oxford English Dictionary*, the word *sacred* is defined as the holy. The sacred includes concept of God, the divine and the transcendent. However, other objects can become sacred or take on an extra-ordinary power by virtue of their association with, or representations of divinity. Sacred objects include time and space (temples), events and transitions (birth and death), materials (cross), cultural products (music, literature), people (saints), social attributes (compassion), psychological attributes (meaning). We would describe persons to be spiritual to the extent they are trying to find, know, experience, or relate to what they perceive as sacred.

The Discovery of the Scared

The search for God begins in childhood. Some scientists have suggested that there is an *innate genetic* basis for spirituality. Others have emphasized that conceptions of God are rooted in the child's intrapsychic capacity to symbolize, fantasize and create superhuman beings. Some have asserted that spirituality grows out of critical life events and challenges that reveal human limitations. And others have emphasized the importance of the social context (familial, institutional, cultural) in shaping the child's understanding of God.

Empirical research on the origins of spirituality is not plentiful. Kirkpatrik suggests that child's mental models of God are likely to correspond to the models of self and others that emerge out of repeat interactions with primary attachment figures (e.g. mother or father)

The Conservation of the Sacred

The search does not end after the sacred has been discovered. Once found, people strive to hold on to the sacred.

There are a number of spiritual methods for conserving the individual's relationship with the sacred. People sustain their relationship by prayer, meditation, and experiencing the spiritual dimension in daily life.

Spirituality offers a unique set of resources for living. Social scientists, health professionals and mental health professionals are striving to develop psychospiritual interventions that integrate spiritual resources into clinical practice.

Chapter 19

Meditation

Meditation actually comprises a family of techniques that go by different names (Zen meditation, Transcendental Meditation, Vipassana meditation) and different categories (concentrative mindfulness, contemplative loving-kindness). The core element that underlies all of them is the cultivation of attention. Of course, you can focus attention in many different ways – for example, nonanalytically and nonemotionally on a single object (on a flame, your breath, a sound, or a single word, such as is done in concentrative meditation, or nonjudgmentally on all thoughts, sights, and sounds without ruminating on them (such as is done in mindfulness meditation), or more broadly by opening yourself to God to contemplate the big questions of life (such as is done in contemplative mediation). Meditation is a personal experience and may be performed in many different ways. Yet certain core elements are recognized:

- Be nonjudgmental. Observe the present moment impartially, with detachment, without evaluation.
- Be nonstriving. Although you are a person committed to goals, don't struggle mentally while meditating.
- Be patient. Don't rush or force things but allow

them to unfold in their own good time.
- Be trusting. Trust yourself and trust that things will work out in life.
- Be open. Pay attention to every little thing, as though you were seeing it for the very first time.
- Let go. Set yourself free of rumination. This is what is called nonattachment.

The Process

Researchers who study the bodies of people during the practice of meditation have confirmed that mediators are able to attain a profound state of physiological rest (indicated by a reduced respiration rate, for instance) and a heightened state of awareness and alertness (indicated by such things as increased blood flow and other relevant markers in the brain). Lyubomirsky (2007) conducted a study in which healthy workers underwent an eight-week training practice in mindfulness meditation. At the end of the eight week those who practiced meditation (compared with a control group) showed increases in their left-frontal cortex, relative to the right. It may be indicated that this particular pattern of greater brain activity in the left versus right part of the brain is observed in happy and approach-oriented individuals. This supports other studies indicating greater happiness and lower depression and anxiety in meditators.

Not surprisingly such physiological effects may translate into and influence a person's health. Meditation interventions have been shown to be effective in patients with heart diseases, chronic pain, skin disorders and a variety of mental health conditions such as depression, anxiety, panic, and substance abuse. Besides these direct benefits, meditation reduces reactivity to stress and boosts self-esteem, positive moods and feelings of control.

A number of intriguing studies have even revealed benefits of meditation for such seemingly intractable characteristics as intelligence, creativity and cognitive flexibility in the elderly.

The Technique

Teachers of meditation advise that mediating involves sitting alone in a comfortable place, back straight. Close your eyes and focus on breathing in and out. As you breathe out, silently repeat a short word (like *one, aum,* or *be*). Or if you prefer, focus on a specific object, sound, or task, like a candle, a tone, or your breath. If your mind wanders (e.g. I have to take my lunch), let your thoughts pass, and then restart by bringing your attention back to your breath. The key is to notice your mind wandering and then to turn inward and "detach" from your thought. Don't let your ruminations and fantasies and plans and memories control you, take charge of them. This will take practice and repetition, beginners usually can only "quiet" or "still" the mind for no more than a few seconds at a time. A common experience is that the moment you think you've emptied your mind, it starts to fill up again.

Build the length of time you are able to meditate from five to twenty minutes and try to do it every day. Ideally arrange for a meditation space. It can be modest or large, decorated – with photos, artworks, or inspirational contents. It should be comfortable and, if possible, free of disattractions.

Meditation has many regards, but it does not come effortlessly Pascal commented" "All of humanity's problems seem from man's inability to sit quietly in a room alone".

Chapter 20

On Inspiration

Inspiration is frequently cited as a source for some of the most significant works and achievements throughout history. People of eminence report experiencing it at various times in their lives. Sometimes it leads to significant changes in oneself; at other times it may lead to new creations or new directions in one's life, work or relationship.

Psychologists, Thrash and Elliot, have noted three core aspects of inspiration: **evocation transcendence** and **approach motivation.** First, inspiration is evoked spontaneously without intention. Inspiration is also transcendent of our animalistic and self-serving concerns and limitations. Such transcendence often involves a moment of clarity and awareness of new possibilities. As Thrash and Elliot observe, *"The height of human motivation spring from the beauty and goodness that precede us and awaken us to better possibilities."* The moment of clarity is often vivid, and can take the form of a grand vision, or "seeing" something one has not seen before. Finally, inspiration involves *approach motivation*, in which the individual strives to transmit, express, or actualize a new idea or vision. Inspiration involves both being inspired by something and acting or that inspiration.

Characteristics of Inspired People

There is a psychological test that measures the frequency with which persons experienced inspiration in their daily lives. Researchers find that inspired people are more open to new experiences and report more absorption in their tasks. "Openness to experience" often come before inspiration, suggesting that those who are more open to inspiration are more likely to experience it. Inspired individuals also report having a strong drive to master their work. Inspired people are more intrinsically motivated and less intrinsically motivated (less motivated by incentives, external awards and perks). Inspiration is less related to variables that involve agency or the enhancement of resources. Therefore, what makes an object inspiring is its perceived subjective intrinsic value, and not how much it is objectively worth or how attainable it is. Inspired people report higher levels of important psychological resources, including belief in their own abilities, self-esteem, and optimism. Mastery of work, absorption, creativity, perceived competence, self-esteem, and optimism are all consequences of inspiration. Interestingly, work mastery comes before inspiration, suggesting that inspiration is not purely passive, it favours the prepared mind.

Inspirations Versus Positive Emotions

Compared to the normal experience of everyday life, inspiration involves elevated levels of positive emotions and task involvement, and lower levels of negative emotions. However, inspiration is not same as positive affect. Compared to being in an enthusiastic and excited state, inspired people report greater levels of spirituality and meaning, and lower levels of volitional control, controllability, and self-responsibility for their inspiration.

Whereas positive affect is activated when someone is making progress towards their immediate, conscious goals, inspiration is more related to an awakening to something new, better, or more important: transcendence of one's previous concerns.

In a recent study, college students were asked to report three goals they intended to accomplish during their semester. They then reported on their progress three times a month. Those who scored higher on inspiration displayed increased goal progress, and their progress was a result of setting more inspired goals. Therefore, people who are generally more inspired in their daily lives also tend to set inspired goals, and these goals are more likely to be successfully attained. Importantly, the relationship between inspiration and goal progress I reciprocal; goal progress predicts future goal inspiration.

Inspiration and Creativity

Inspired people view themselves as more creative and show actual increases in self-ratings of creativity over time. Patent-holding inventors report being inspired more frequently and intensely than non-patent holders. The higher the frequency of inspiration, the higher is the number of patents hold. Being in a state of inspiration also predicts the creativity of writing samples across scientific writing, poetry, and fiction. Inspired writers are more efficient and productive, and spend less time in pausing and more time writing. The link between inspiration and creativity is consistent with the transcendent aspect of inspiration, since creativity involves seeing possibility beyond existing constraints. Importantly inspiration and effort predict different aspects of an activity. Individuals who exert more effort writing spend more of their time pausing, delete more words, write more sentences per paragraph, and have better technical merit and use of rhyming in poems, but their work is not considered more creative.

Increasing Wellness

Inspirational effect is not transitory; it predicts life satisfaction. Inspiration matters a lot. However, one should not put pressure on oneself to become inspired. The key scientific finding suggests that inspiration is not willed – it happens. This does not mean inspiration is completely outside our control. Inspiration is best thought of as a surprising interaction between our current knowledge and the information we receive from the world. Research shows clearly that preparation (work mastery) is a key ingredient. While inspiration is not the same as effort, effort is an essential condition for inspiration, preparing the mind for an inspirational experience.

Openness to experience and positive affect are also important, as having an open mind and approach-oriented attitude will make it more likely that we will be aware of the inspiration once it arrives. Small accomplishments are also important, setting off a productive and creative cycle.

Another incredibly important, and often overlooked trigger of inspiration is exposure to inspiring leaders, role models, heroes, coaches and mentors. Such exposure moves recipient to transcend normal preoccupations and everyday concerns. Of-course, a topic like inspiration requires further scientific exploration for the use of the construct in the direction of individual and social enrichment.

Chapter 21

Performance Excellence

The defining slogan in the modern workplace is more, bigger, faster. There are more customers to please, more e-mails to answer, more phone calls to return, more tasks to do, more meetings to attend, and more places to visit. The technologies that make instant communication possible anywhere, at any time, speed up decision making, create efficiencies, and fuel a global market place. But too much of a thing may become a bad thing. Left unmanaged and unregulated, these same technologies have the potential to overwhelm us. The relentless urgency that characterizes most corporate cultures undermines creativity, quality, engagement, thoughtful deliberation, productivity, and ultimately, performance.

The consulting firm Towers Perrin's most recent global workplace study bears this out. Conducted in 2007-2008, before the worldwide recession, it looked at some 90,000 employees in eighteen countries. Only 20 percent of them felt fully engaged, 40 percent were enrolled, and 38 percent were disengaged. More than a hundred studies have demonstrated similar gloomy picture of the modern era.

The Ericsson Study

In 1993, Anders Ericsson, a leading researcher

in expert performance and a professor in Florida State University, conducted an extraordinary study designed to explore the power of practice among violinists. Ericsson divided thirty young violinists at the Music Academy of Berlin into three separate groups, based on ratings from their professors.

The "best" group consisted of those destined to eventually become professional soloists. The "good" violinists were those expected to have careers playing as part of orchestras. The third group, recruited from the academy, was headed for careers as music teachers. All three groups had begun playing violin around the age of eight.

Vast amount of data was collected on each of the participants. All participants kept diary of their activities, hour by hour, over the course of an entire week. They were also asked to rate each hour's primary activity on three measures using a scale of 1 to 10. The first one was how important the activity was to improve their performance on the violin. The second was how difficult they found it to do. The third was how intrinsically enjoyable they found the activity.

The top two groups, both destined for professional careers, turned out to practice an average of twenty-four hours a week. The future music teachers, by contrast, put in just over nine hours, or about a third of the amount of time as the top two groups. This difference was undeniably dramatic and does suggest how much practice matters. But equally fascinating was the relationship Ericsson found between practice and intermittent rest.

All of the thirty violinists agreed that "practice alone" had the biggest impact on improving their performance as violinists. On an average, those on the top two groups slept 8 – 6 hours a day – nearly an hour longer than those in the music teacher group. The top two groups also took considerably more daytime naps than did the lower-rated group.

Great performance, Ericsson Study suggests, work more intensely than most of us do but also recover more deeply. The best violinists figured out, intuitively, that they generated the highest return on their investment by working intensely, without interruption, for no more than ninety minutes at a time and no more than 4 hours a day. They also recognized it was essential to take time, intermittently, to rest and refuel.

It is important to recognize that doing an activity for a long time is no guarantee that one will do it well.

We are not meant to rest solely at night. Basic rest activity cycle implies the ninety-minute period during which we move through the five stages of sleep. It is suggested that we experience a parallel ninety-minute cycle in our working life. At night, we move from light to deep sleep. During the day, we oscillate every ninety minutes or so from higher to lower alertness. We call these "ultradian" cycle, which literally means "less than a day".

Chapter 22

Seeking Uniqueness

Every person is like all other persons.
Every person is like some other persons.
Every person is like none other person.

These lines of anthropologists capture an essential element of human behaviour. Among other things, it is also revealed that people have a need to be distinctive and special. Of course, people also have need for similarity. These needs for distinctiveness and similarity oppose one another in the sense that satisfaction of one enhances the potency of the other. Accordingly, people find a compromise position of intermediate level of self-distinctiveness more satisfying than either extreme similarity or extreme dissimilarity relative to other persons.

It is posited that people seek to establish and maintain a sense of moderate self-distinctiveness, because perceptions of either extreme similarity or extreme dissimilarity to others are experienced as being unpleasant. Accordingly, people should be happiest when perceiving that they are moderately different relative to others. In a test of this prediction, students were given feedback about how similar their responses in a lifestyle survey were to those of other respondents and then they were asked about their moods. As predicted, the students who were told that they were moderately similar to other respondents reported more positive moods than those students who were told they were either highly similar or highly dissimilar to other respondents.

Although we do not have potential explanations for individual difference in the strength of uniqueness, there are two plausible hypotheses. First, it is reasoned that the need for uniqueness arises because people are moderately different from one another and have learned to perceive themselves accordingly. This self-image takes on motivational properties because people need a stable self-concept.

Some individuals may possess salient personal attributes that are more unusual than those of others and therefore, may come to see themselves as more distinctive than others. Those self-perceptions, in turn, may influence the level of self-distinctiveness that individuals find most desirable. Consistent with the possibility, researchers have found an especially strong need for uniqueness among people whose name or family circumstances are likely to make them experience a sense of specialness. Specifically, evidence of a higher than what need for uniqueness has been found among women with unusual names, students who are firstborn or only children, and children of interfaith marriages.

Second, people learn to value uniqueness in environments that encourage freedom and reward independence. Thus, individual and group differences in the need for uniqueness may reflect different environmental backgrounds and reinforcement histories. In other words, if uniqueness seeking is rewarded in a culture, this tendency is strengthened in that cultural system.

In contrast, people prefer a moderate level of self-distinctiveness because they have needs for social acceptance and approval. Consistent with this expectation, uniqueness is negatively related to social anxiety, shyness and susceptibility to normative influences.

There are visible benefits of uniqueness seeking. The establishment of a sense of uniqueness is emotionally satisfying to individuals. Many people seek psychiatric help to identify and promote their individual distinctiveness.

In addition to promoting the psychological welfare of individuals, uniqueness seeking benefits society by promoting diversity. As people seek to differentiate themselves from others, they pursue different interests and goals. The diffusion of pursuits reduces competition and conflict over limited resources. It also creates entirely new areas of success for people in general.

As people seek to differentiate themselves from others, they also develop different attitudes, beliefs, knowledge bases and skills. This diversity of human resource is an asset of immense value. Across many domains of achievement, diversity of resources and efforts has increased the likelihood of human success.

Chapter 23

Cultural Intelligence

In a world where crossing boundaries is routine, *cultural intelligence* becomes vitally important attitude and skill, and not just for interactional bankers and borrowers. Anyone who forms a new company spends the first few weeks deciphering its cultural code. Within any company there are subcultures as well. The sales force can't talk to the engineers, and the public relation people lose patience with the lawyers. Each has a constellation of manners, meanings, histories and values that well confuse the interloper and cause him or her to stumble. Unless he or she has a high *cultural intelligence quotient or CQ.*

Cultural intelligence is related to emotional intelligence, but it picks up where emotional intelligence leaves off. A person with high emotional intelligence grasps what makes us human and at the same time what makes each of us different from one another. A person with high cultural intelligence can somewhat tense out of a person's or grasp's behaviour those features that would be true of all people and all groups, and those that are neither universal no idiosyncratic. The vast realm that lies between these two poles is culture.

The central element that cultural intelligence and emotional intelligence do share is a propensity to suspend judgment to think before acting. For someone richly endowed with CQ, the suspension might take hours or days, while someone with low CQ might have to take weeks or months. In either case, it involves using your senses to register all the ways that the personalities interacting in front of you are different from those in your home culture yet similar to one another.

Although some aspect of cultural intelligence is innate, anyone reasonably alert, motivated and poised can affirm an acceptable level of cultural intelligence. The cultivation of cultural intelligence corresponds to the three components of cultural intelligence: *the cognitive, the physical and the emotional/ motivational*. Cultural intelligence resides in the *body* and the *heart*, as well as the *head*. Although most managers are not equally strong in all the three areas, each faculty is seriously hampered without the other two.

Learning about the briefs, customs and taboos of foreign cultures will never prepare a person for every situation that arises. However, a newcomer needs to device what we call learning strategies. Although most people find it difficult to discover a point of entry into alien cultures, an individual with high cognitive CQ notices clues to a culture's shared understandings. For example, a person may look for consistencies in the various individuals' traits and eventually determines that they are all punctual, deadline- oriented and tolerant of unconventional manners. From that he/ she is able to infer much about the character of people in new culture. This is where head plays its role.

Of course, you will not convince foreign hosts, guests or colleagues simply by showing you understand their culture. Your action must prove that you have already to some extent entered their world. Whether it is the way you shake hands or order a coffee, evidence of an ability to mirror the customs and gestures of the people around you well prove that you esteem them well enough to want to be like them. By adopting people's habits and mannerisms, you eventually come to understand in the most elemental way what it is like to be them. They, in turn, become more trusting and open.

An important indicator of the physical component involves interpersonal space. Americans and western Europeans do not feel comfortable standing in a close physical proximity. Consequently the appropriate manipulation of such body language is indicative of one's cultural intelligence.

Finally, the role of heart is equally important. Adapting to a new culture involves overcoming obstacles and setbacks. People can do that only if they believe in their efficacy. If successful in the face of challenging situations in the past, their confidence grew. Confidence is always rooted in mastery of a particular task or set of circumstances.

A person who does not believe himself/herself capable of understanding people from unfamiliar cultures will often give up after his/her efforts meet hostility or incomprehension. By contrast, a person with high motivation will, upon confronting obstacles, setbacks, or even failures, reengage with greater vigor. To stay motivated, highly efficacious people do not depend on obtaining rewards.

While the three components of cultural intelligence (head, body and heart) have their specific roles, they work together in people with high cultural intelligence. Unlike other aspects of personality, cultural intelligence can be developed in psychologically healthy and professionally competent people.

Chapter 24

Forgiveness

Gratitude and forgiveness are commonly used in everyday language. Emmons (2004) defines gratitude as "a sense of thankfulness and joy in response to receiving a gift, whether the gift can be a tangible benefit from a specific other or a moment of peaceful bliss evoked by natural beauty". Furthermore, gratitude is experienced when a motivationally relevant, congruent, and/or desirable outcome is received and attributed to the efforts of another.

Forgiveness, on the other hand is defined as the framing of a perceived transgression such that one's attachment to the transgressor, transgression, and the sequel of the transgression is transformed from negative to neutral or positive. The source of a transgression, and therefore the object of forgiveness may be oneself, another person or persons, or a situation that one views as being one's control. (Yamhure-Thompson & Snyder, 2003)

Definition of forgiveness vary in two major ways. First, forgiveness varies to the extent that it incorporates active benevolence, prosocial change, or even love and appreciation towards the source of transgression (passive tolerance, ceasing to blame, or a reduced sense of victimization). Second, reconciliation is considered to be an integral component of forgiveness.

Although many people view gratitude and forgiveness as two separate concepts, it is more appropriate to consider them as two sides of the same, precious coin. On one side, grateful individuals choose to focus on and appreciate the positives in their lives, including their own and others' strength, talents, gifts, and prosocial behaviours, as well as favourable events. This gratitude tends to promote and maintain a positive view of one-self, others and situational factors and events. On the other side of the coin, forgiveness is a positive approach in dealing with the negative in one's life, including faults, vulnerabilities, and negative behaviours and outcomes that are perceived in oneself, others, and situational factors and events. However, by forgiving, one is taking a positive stance with oneself or others. To forgive means to accept that the future can be more effectively optimized if one does not dwell on the negatives of the past.

A combination of gratitude and forgiveness can help shape perceptions and attributions and instill a proactive approach of *positive labeling* and *positive identity* that can enhance one's bank of psychological capital. For example, carrying negative thoughts about another such as revenge, draws down the positivity of individuals and, in turn, decreases strength. We can argue that revenge consumes the individual in negativity, taking attention away from things that are positive.

Forgiveness is facilitated and capitalized on by gratitude as transgressions are positively appraised as opportunities to learn important lessons in life. Then, from the accelerating forgiveness, one's gratitude is intensified towards other more favourable relationship and situations and the upward spiral of positivity continues. Forgiveness allows the victim to view the transgressor in a more positive light, resulting in enhancing the possibility for seeing through and being grateful for the positives and the lessons to be learned from that person or event.

Further Benefits of Gratitude

Gratitude is a moral emotion for three reasons. First, the experience of gratitude lets us know that we have been behaving in a prosocial way towards others. Second, it motivates us to engage in prosocial behaviours and inhibits antisocial behaviour. Third, it reinforces moral behaviours in the person who has acted in the benevolent way to whom we have expressed our gratitude.

Gratitude is also good for our health. Emmons and Shelton (2003) have shown in a series of studies that people who kept diaries of events for which they were grateful showed improved health and subjective well-being compared with people who kept diaries of stresses or other types of events within their day-to-day lives.

Forgiveness and Atonement

Betrayal, breaches of trust, acts of physical or psychological hostility all occur within friendship and other relationships. Spirals of retributions and retaliations which culminate in the destruction of relationships may follow. Forgiveness and atonement are important ways for curbing such escalating spirals.

Forgiveness is a personal prosocial response to an acknowledged transgression for which the transgressor was clearly responsible. With forgiveness, we say to the transgressor, "I acknowledge that you made a transgression against one, but I am not going to seek, retribution, because I forgive you". With forgiveness, the debt created by the transgression is cancelled. Forgiveness is distinct from legal pardoning, since it is a personal response to a breach in a relationship rather than the result of a legal process. Forgiveness is distinct from condoning or justifying the transgression, rationalizing or excusing the transgression as aring from extenuating circumstances, denying the seriousness of the transgression. Atonement, in contrast, is the contrite acknowledgement of wrongdoing by a transgressor and making reparation for wrongdoing or injury to another person. With atonement, we say, 'I acknowledge that I have hurt you, I am sorry for that, and I will make amends for my transgression'. Together, forgiveness and atonement are ways of repairing relationships that have been damaged by transgression.

Forgiveness can lead to improved psychological and physical well-being and to a deepening of the relationship with the transgressor. Alongside these benefits, there are barriers to the expression of forgiveness. We may feel that our forgiveness will be interpreted as a sign of weakness and that this will lead to repeated transgressions.

Atonement, too, has its benefits. When we atone for transgressions we reduce our feelings of guilt and may also elicit forgiveness. Atonement and forgiveness may also improve psychological and physical well-being. However, there are barriers to atonement. Atonement entails acknowledging personal responsibility for wrongdoing, experiencing the feelings of guilt and shame that go with this acknowledgement.

Both forgiveness and atonement require us to put pride aside and be humble. Humility involves seeing oneself as no better or no worse than others.

As indicated earlier, forgiveness is associated with better psychological and physical well-being. Laboratory studies also support the link between forgiveness and well-being. In an experimental analogue study researcher found that participants showed for greater arousal as indexed by heart-rate, blood pressure and skin conductance in situation where they mentally rehearsed non-forgiving responses to transgressors compared with situations where they mentally rehearsed forgiving responses. Interventions that increase forgiveness enhance psychological and physical well-being. Compared with controls, hostile heart-attack survivors who learned how to adopt a forgiving attitude showed a reduction in hostility and heart problems after an intervention programme which aimed to promote relaxation, forgiveness and a balanced lifestyle.

Forgiveness has an important role to play in marital adjustment. Sometimes marital psychotherapists use the Gestalt therapy empty chair technique. Such therapy involves engaging in an imaginal dialogue with the transgressor. During this dialogue there is an acceptance into awareness of strong feelings of anger and sadness associated with the transgression; a letting go of unmet interpersonal needs arising from the transgression; the development of empathy for the transgressor; and the construction of a new way of conceptualizing the self and the transgressor. In marital therapy where partners have hurt each other, facilitating forgiveness and atonement may be central to helping couples break out of destructive repetitive patterns of interaction which maintain their marital distress.

Chapter 25

Humility

Although humility is commonly equated with a sense of unworthiness and low self-regard, true humility is a rich multi- faceted construct that is characterized by an accurate assessment of one's characteristic, an ability to acknowledge limitations and a "forgetting of the self".

However, humility has been neglected in research for long. Two factors come readily to mind. First, the concept of humility is linked to values and religion in many people's minds. A second factor undoubtedly contributing to the neglect of humility is the lack of a well–established measure of this construct.

A challenge facing psychologists interested in the construct of humility involves the variation in definition. For many, humility simply means holding oneself in low self-regard. For example, the *Oxford English Dictionary* (1998), humility is defined as the "the quality of being humble or having lowly opinion of oneself, meekness, lowliness, humbleness; opposite of pride or haughtiness." From this "low self - esteem" perspective, humility certainly does not stand out of the more attractive virtues.

In reality humility is antithesis of this definition. To be humble is not to have a low opinion of oneself, it is to have an accurate opinion of oneself. It is the ability to keep one's talents and accomplishments in perspective, to have a sense of self–acceptance, and to be free from arrogance and low self–esteem.

Humility is not self-deprecation. It represents wisdom. It is knowing you were created with special talents and abilities to share with the world. But it can also be an understanding that you are one of many souls created by God, and each has an important role to play in life. Humility is knowing you are smart, but not all knowing. It is accepting that you have personal power, but you are not omnipotent. Humility makes us receptive. It leaves us more open to learn from others. The opposite of humility is arrogance – the belief that we are wiser or better than others. Arrogance promotes separation rather that community.

For many, there is a religious dimension to humility – the recognition that "God infinitely exceeds anything anyone has ever said of Him and that He is beyond human comprehension and understanding". Here too, emphasis is not one unworthiness and inadequacy but on the notion of a higher, greater power. It has the implication, that although we may have considerable wisdom and knowledge, there always are limits to our perspective. Humility carries with it an open – mindedness, a willingness to admit mistakes and seek advice, and a desire to learn.

Also inherent in the state of humility is a relative lark of self–focus or self–pre–occupation. Psychologists refer to the process of becoming "unselved", which goes hand in hand with the recognition of one's place in the world. A person who has sense of humility is no longer at the centre of his or her world. The focus is on the larger community of which he or she is one part Consider the person who repeatedly protests, "Oh! I am not really good in literature." Such humble protests betray a marked self–focus.

In relinquishing the very human tendency towards self-focus, persons with humility become more and more open to recognizing the abilities, potential, worth and importance of others. One important consequence of becoming "unselved" is that we no longer have the need to enhance and define an all–important self at the expense of others or out-evaluation of others. Humility is an increase in the evaluation of others and not a decrease in the evaluation of oneself.

There are a few other concepts which are mistakened to be similar to humility. The concept of modesty focuses primarily on a moderate estimate of personal merits or achievements. As such, modestly does not capture the essence of humility such as forgetting of the self and an appreciation of the variety ways in which others can be worthy. Rather, use of the term modesty often extends into issues of propriety in behaviour and dress, where humility is relevant. This modesty is too narrow missing fundamental components of humility, and too broad, relating also to bodily exposure and other dimensions of propriety.

The construct of narcissism is perhaps most related to humility. People who are narcissistic clearly lack humility. In conceptualizing narcissisms, social psychologists tend to focus on grandiosity, an exaggerated sense of self-importance, and overestimation of one's abilities. Narcissistic individuals clearly lack many other essential components of humility. But it is not clear that people who score low on measures of narcissism necessarily embody humility.

Humility offers a number of benefits. A sense of humility inhibits anger and aggression and fosters forgiveness. People like and feel less threatened by other who are modest about their achievements, whereas boastful arrogant behaviour often results in social disapproval.

Clinicians have long noted the links between excessive self-focus and a broad range of psychological symptoms, including anxiety, depression, social phobias and so on. There are many advantages to "escaping the self", not the least of which is a relief from the burden of self-preoccupation.

Chapter 26

Rewire Your Brain and Be Happy

Everyone seeks happiness, but a few individuals succeed in experiencing sustainable happiness. In the enactment of life's drama, the trichotomy of brain, mind and behaviour complicates the scenarios. Many people and even many scientists believe that the human brain is the finest product of the evolutionary process and the subtle script it carries directs the activities of our mind and diversity of our behaviour. Essentially every person is like all other humans, though every person is similar to some other humans to some extent and the person is similar to a few person to a small extent.

The brain provides commonality to human behaviour. In fact, human brain a combination of three brains: a unicellular brain, a mammalian brain and a human brain. Because of the unicellular brain as possessed by unicellular organisms, we are responsive to simple reflexes, such as moving away from a hot object. Our mammalian brain is helpful in guiding us to do a number of voluntary actions. But the most evolved and most recent brain is the neo-cortex or neo-brain that is distinctively human. If we plan to get up at an unusual hour of 4 am just because we have to catch a bus, we rarely fail. Even if our usual habit is to get up at 6 am in the morning, the auto-suggestion of getting at 4 am works fine with us. The neo-cortex registers the suggestion and we get some sort of signal, such as an unusual dream, to get up. This distinctive property of guiding our behaviour is uniquely human.

Although human brain is endowed with unique properties, there are dogmas in the world of brain science. One persistent dogma is that the adult brain is essentially fixed in form and function. The dogma is wrong. Instead, the brain has the property of neuroplasticity, the ability to change the structure and pattern of activity in significant ways not only in childhood, which is not very surprising, but also in adulthood and throughout life. The change can come about as a result of experiences we have as well of purely internal activity – our thoughts.

Experiences may take various forms. The brains of people who have been blind from birth and who learn to read by Braille, the writing system based on tiny raised dots that the finger slide across experience a measurable increase in the size and activity of the motor cortex and somatosensory cortex that control movement and receive tactile sensation from the reading fingers. Even more dramatically, their visual cortex – which is normally hardwired to process signals from the eyes and turn them into visual images – undertakes a career change and takes on the job of processing sensation from the fingers rather than the input from the eyes.

Reading braille is an example of intense, repeated sensory and learning experience of the outside world. But the brain can change in response to messages generated internally (our thoughts and intentions). These changes can increase or decrease the cortical real estate devoted to specific functions. Similarly, thoughts alone can increase or decrease activity in specific brain circuits that underlie psychological illness, as when the therapy quiets the overactivity of the "worry circuit" which causes obsessive–compulsive disorder (OCD). Through mental activity alone, which itself is a produce of the brain, we can intentionally change our brain.

The Cortical Representation

The idea that there is a one-to-one correspondence between structure and function dates back 1862 when French anatomist Paul Broca announced that he had identified the brain region that produces speech. It is an area towards the back of the frontal lobes. He concluded from autopsy of a man who had lost essentially all the powers of speech. The brain's speech producing area is called the Broca's area.

With this discovery, other brain scientists joined the race of identifying particular brain area for particular function. A German neurologist Korbinian Brodmann, yielded structure function relationship for fifty-two distinct regions. For example, Brodmann number 1 represents the parts of somatosensory cortex that processes tactile sensation from specific spots in the skin. Brodmann area number 52 represents parainsular region where the temporal lobe and insula meet. The visual cortex is known as Brodmann area number 17. Area number 10 is the front-most part of the prefrontal cortex which has increased most in size over the course of evolution and seems to allow us in multi task.

No region of the brain has been as precisely mapped as the somatosensory cortex. This strip of cortex runs roughly over the top of the brain from ear to ear. The left somatosensory cortex receives signal from the right and vice versa. Each part of the body is assigned a particular spot in the somatosensory cortex for processing. As a result, the somatosensory cortex is essentially a map of the body

– one that would give Google mappers a heart attack. In experiments in the 1960s, Canadian neurosurgeon Wilder Penfield stimulated systematically different spots of somatosensory cortex and participants reported sensation in different parts of the body in this way. Penfield was able to "map" the somatosensory cortex assigning each spot a corresponding part of the body.

There is an element of humour in cortical representation. Although the hand is below the arm, the somatosensory hand abuts the region that receives signal from the face. Similarly, the somatosensory representation of the genitals lies directly below the feet. It is observed that with more cortical space, a body part becomes more sensitive. The tip of our tongue, which has a larger representation can feel the ridges of our teeth, whereas the backs of our hands have smaller somatosensory representation.

Because of the past works, the belief was strengthened and carried forward into the idea that particular activity must also be hardwired and if not strictly unchangeable, atleast persistent. According to this view, mental illness such as depression might be caused by underactivity in some area of the prefrontal cortex and overactivity in the amygdala and the underlying biology is as permanent as your finger prints.

Towards the Plasticity Notion

However, more recently there has been change in the structure-function relationship. Edward Taub and his associates initiated a bold series of experiments, known as the **Silver Spring Experiments,** in the Institute of Behavioural Research Silver Spring (Maryland, USA). The neural centres representing sensory connection to fingers were severed in monkeys. Animals lost all sensation in those limbs. Although the case sparked animal right movement in the USA and Taub had to face criminal investigation, the result of these sensory deprivation studies in 1991 was stunning in the sense it shattered the fixed notion of hardwiring. The region of monkey's somatosensory cortex which originally processed sensation from the fingers, hands and arms had changed jobs. As a result of receiving no signals from body parts, the region now processed signals from the face instead. The amount of brain now receiving sensations from the face had grown to fourteen square millimeters – a "massive cortical reorganization".

Around the same time, other studies of monkeys showed that adult primate brain can change in response to something much less extreme than amputation or nerve-cutting strategy. In the seminal study, scientists at the University of California, San Francisco trained owl monkeys to develop an acute sense of touch in their fingers. They were trained to brush a spinning disk. Day in and day out, monkeys underwent this exercise, until they had done it hundreds of times. The region of their brain – specifically in somatosensory cortex – that received signals from the finger had been trained to feel the grooves in the spinning disks. Structure-function relationships are not hardwired. Instead, the physical lay-out of the brain – how much space it assigns to which tasks and body parts – is shaped by how an organism behaves.

Seeing the Thunder, Hearing the Lightening

The place to look into the application of findings obtained from animal research involves the study of sensory experiences from those who are blind or deaf. The brain is capable of bigger reorganization. Studies of blind and deaf examined much bigger chunks of neural real estate: the visual cortex which occupies nearly one-third of the brain's volume. It is nestled towards the back and the auditory cortex, which stretches across the top of the brain across the ears. We are familiar with a folk wisdom that the blind has especially sharp hearing and the deaf has especially sharp eye sight. But the folk wisdom is not cent percent true. In fact, blind people do not hear softer sounds, and deaf people cannot detect minimal contrasts or see in dimmer light than hearing people can. But compensation works in another way.

In people who are deaf from birth, objects in the peripheral vision are perceived not only in the visual cortex but also in the auditory cortex. **The auditory cortex sees**. It is as if the auditory cortex, tired of enforced inactivity as a result of receiving no signals from the ears, take upon itself as a regimen of job retraining, so that it now processes visual signals. This has practical consequences. Deaf people are faster and more accurate at detecting the movements of objects in their peripheral vision than are hearing people.

Something comparable happens in people who are blind from birth or an early age. In them, no signals reach the visual cortex. However, the visual cortex does not go waste. In blind people who become proficient in reading, Braille, the visual cortex switches jobs to processing tactile signal from those reading fingers. This discovery was so unexpected that some of neuroscience's most eminent practitioners refused to believe it. As a consequence, the submission turned down by *Science* was published by its arch competitor *Nature* (April 1996).

The brains of the blind change in another way too. When they use their peripheral hearing – to locate the source of a sound, for instance, something they tend to be better at than sighted people – they use their visual cortex. Their brains have gone what we call compensatory reorganization. As a result, **the visual cortex hears**. Once again, William James proved prescient. A century before these discoveries, in his 1892 book *Psychology: The Briefer course*, he wondered whether if neurons get crossed inside the brain, *"we should hear the lightening and see the thunder"* ---- a foreshadowing of the profound alternation in the brain's primary sensory cortices that can result from experience.

In brief, the brain can change assigning a new function to a region that originally did something else. These conclusions were derived from studies conducted on the blind and the deaf. What about normal population?

Pascual-Leone conducted experiments involving "virtual piano players". It was shown that merely thinking about players' keyboard exercise expanded the region of motor cortex devoted to moving fingers. In another bold experiment, Pascual-Leone recruited healthy volunteers to spend five days in a safe experiment at Beth Israel Deaconess Medical Center in Boston. The participants were blindfolded. To keep from dying of boredom they were provided with sensorially intense activity learning Braille and fine-tuning their hearing. Prior to experimental intervention, they were subjected to fMRI scans. At the end of the five days of such exercise, they were subjected to scans. When they heard something the activity in their visual cortex increased. The visual cortex is supposed to handle sight. Yet, after a mere five days of an unusual sensory activity, scans indicated a radical change in function.

If the visual cortex, which seems like the most hardwired of all the brain's hardwired regions, can so quickly alter its function as a result of sensory input and sensory deprivation, surely it is time to question how much the brain is really fixed and unchangeable. In all likelihood the visual cortex did not grow new connections to the ears and fingers, five days wasn't time enough for that Pascual-Leone suspects that instead "some rudimentary somatosensory and auditory connections to the visual cortex must already be present," left over from the period of brain development when neurons from the eyes and ears and fingers connect to many regions of the cortex rather than just the ones they're supposed to. When input from the retina to the visual cortex ceased because of the blindfold, the other sensory connections were unmasked. Even neural cables that receive no traffic for decades can start carrying signals again.

Therapeutic Application

The realization that sensory experiences can rewire the brain has had important real-world consequences. From the discovery that a region of the brain could be retrained to perform a new function, it is inferred that people in whom a stroke has damaged one region of the brain could train a healthy region of their brain to assume the function of the damaged part. The method of treatment is called **constraint-induced movement therapy.**

The therapy could be explained with the example in whom a stroke has damaged a region of the motor cortex, leaving one arm paralyzed. The therapist would put this patient's good arm in a sling and her good hand in an oven mitt for about 90 percent of waking hours for about two weeks, so she could not use either, leaving her no choice but to try to use her paralyzed arm in activities of daily living and the rehabilitation exercise advised. These exercises, six hours a day for two five-day weeks, involved intensive use of the paralyzed arm, which was actually slightly functional. The patients manipulate cups and eating utensils. After scores of hours of practice, most patients make huge improvements.

Brain plasticity can take several forms. Plasticity is an intrinsic property of the human brain. The potential of the adult brain to reprogram itself might be much greater than has previously been assumed. Neuroplasticity allows the brain to break the bonds of its own genome, which dictates that one region will "see" and another will "hear". The genetical guided blueprint is fine for most people under most conditions, but not all of us all the time – not when we lose our sight or suffer a stroke. **The brain is neither immutable nor static, but continuously remodeled by the lives we lead.**

Mind over Matter
1. **The revolution in neuroplasticity shows that brain can change as a result of the distinct inputs.**
2. **Brain can change as result of the experiences we have in this world – how we move and behave and what sensory signals arrive in our cortex.**
3. **The brain changes in response to purely mental activity, ranging from mediation to cognitive (thought) restructuring.**

Recommended Readings

Bandura, A. (1997). *Self-efficacy*. New York: Free Press

Baumgardner, S.R. & Crothers, M.K. (2009). Positive psychology. Delhi: Pearson Education

Carr, A. (2004). *Positive psychology*. New York: Routledge

Davidson, R.J. & Begley, S. (2012). *The emotional life of your brain*. London: Hodder

Goleman, D. (1995). *Emotional intelligence*. New York: Bantam Books

Goleman, D. (2013). *Focus: The hidden driver of excellence*. New Delhi: Bloomsbury

Luthans, F., Youssef-Morgan, C.M. & Avolio, B.J. (2015). *Psychological capital and beyond*. New Delhi: Oxford University Press

Sahoo, F.M. (2004). *Sex roles in transition*. Delhi: Kalpaz Publication.

Sahoo, F.M. (2021). *Melody of mind*. Dublin, USA: Black Eagle Book

Sahoo, F.M., Tripathy, S. & Sahoo, K. (2021). *Happiness flows*. Dublin, OH, USA: Black Eagle Books.

Seligman, M.E.P (1991). *Learned optimism*. New York: Knopf

Snyder, C.R. & Lopez, S.J. (2005). *Handbook of positive psychology*. New York: Oxford University Press

Snyder, C.R., Lopez, S.J. & Pedrotti, J.T. (2011). Positive psychology. New Delhi: Sage

About the Book

The book *Dynamics of Personal Growth* is a precious gem to be treasured for personal growth and development. It offers the latest scientific research including positive psychology finding and neuroscientific tips. It answers deep-rooted questions.

- What is the secret of building self-confidence?
- How can we develop the habit of looking at the brighter side of things?
- What is the mechanism of bouncing back from adversity?
- How can we enhance emotional intelligence?
- Who are free of gender stereotypes?
- When do we achieve genuine growth and development?
- Why do some people attain success while other falter?

And many more questions _____

Black Eagle Books

www.blackeaglebooks.org
info@blackeaglebooks.org

Black Eagle Books, an independent publisher, was founded as a nonprofit organization in April, 2019. It is our mission to connect and engage the Indian diaspora and the world at large with the best of works of world literature published on a collaborative platform, with special emphasis on foregrounding Contemporary Classics and New Writing.

www.ingramcontent.com/pod-product-compliance
Lightning Source LLC
Chambersburg PA
CBHW020524080526
44583CB00013B/727